THE WORLD'S GREATEST
UFO SIGHTINGS

Photograph Acknowledgements

Fortean Picture Library 70, 76, 88, 94, 95, 96 top, 96 bottom, 98, 99, 102, 103, 104, 108, 112, 114, 116, 117, 120, 129, 130 top, 131, 132, 134, 136/Klaus Aarsleff 137 top/Janet & Colin Bord 130 bottom/Michael Buhler 82/Paul Devereux 137 bottom/Philippa Foster 18/Llewellyn Publications 121/ Denis Stacy 21, 143, 147, 151//Dezsö Sternoczky/SUFOI 119/Clas Svahn 109, 111

THE WORLD'S GREATEST UFO SIGHTINGS

Nigel Cawthorne

This 2002 edition published by Chancellor Press,
an imprint of Bounty Books, a division of
Octopus Publishing Group Ltd.,
2–4 Heron Quays, London E14 4JP

Reprinted 2002

ISBN 0 7537 0563 X

A CIP catalogue record for this book is available from
the British Library

Printed in England by Mackays of Chatham

Contents

1 Lights in the Sky

Encounters with Flying Triangles

Flying saucers have developed a lot since they were first spotted in 1947. In the aftermath of that incident nearly all UFOs seen were saucer shaped. Later, cigar shapes became more common. Although both disc-shaped craft and cylindrical UFOs are still around, the latest batch, seen since the 1980s, are three-sided craft. These Flying Triangles were responsible for the biggest mass sighting in history.

The first major wave of sightings of Flying Triangles occurred in the Hudson Valley area of upstate New York and Connecticut in March 1983. Witnesses reported seeing 'V-shaped' UFOs, and often referred to them as 'flying wings'. They were extremely large, over three hundred feet in length. One eyewitness said the unidentified craft was 'so huge it filled up the entire sky', and others described them as being larger than a football field but with multicoloured flashing lights.

They only appeared triangular when viewed from the ground. Seen in profile from the air they were flat, some reports described them as being wedge-shaped or shaped like a boomerang – though some mistakenly said they were circular. Nevertheless most witnesses reported sightings of solid objects made up of some type of very dark, gun-metal grey material. Such objects have been seen by at least five thousand witnesses worldwide, including police officers and scientists. All indicate that these UFOs, which are often the silent, slow-moving type, were like nothing they had ever seen before.

One distinctive feature of these craft is the three red lights mounted on the underside. There is one light at each corner, though many witnesses report a fourth bright white light in the middle of the configuration. Unlike aircraft identification lights, the Flying Triangle's lights do not appear to flash.

A flash in the sky often precedes the appearance of Flying Triangles and they sometimes project a beam of light onto the ground. They can accelerate and decelerate more rapidly than conventional aircraft and change direction in an instant, and they are silent, apart from a low humming sound. Electrical disturbances are also associated with their appearance.

Between 1983 and 1987, hundreds of people saw these triangular craft in the Hudson Valley area. However, UFO sightings are so common in the US that few people outside UFO circles took any notice. It was only when Flying Triangles began appearing over Belgium in 1989 and 1990 that the world took them seriously.

The Belgian wave of sightings began on 29 November 1989. At dusk on that evening, two Sergeant Majors of the Belgian Gendarmerie were on patrol, travelling down the road from Eupen to Kittenis in the Hautes Fagnes region of eastern Belgium, when they noticed something strange, two hundred yards away to one side of the road. A slowly moving object was hovering, around a thousand feet above a field next to the road.

Both policemen noted that it was a dark triangular craft with three powerful lights shining from its underside onto the ground below. In the centre, it had a coloured light that changed from red to orange and back again.

Suddenly the object turned towards them and passed directly over their vehicle. As it did so, it illuminated the whole area. When directly above them, its triangle form was all the more obvious. They also noted that the craft appeared almost completely noiseless, except for a very soft humming sound.

It travelled slowly towards Eupen, then stopped motionless, hovering above the dam at Gileppe for a period of forty-five minutes. After that it moved away in the direction of Baelen and Spa, where it disappeared.

The two gendarmes contacted the Royal Belgian Air Force base at Bierset, which, like the radar stations at Glons and Butgenbach, had already detected an anomalous blip on their radar screens.

These radar reports were positive readings made by skilled operatives, who would not have misinterpreted reflections from thermal inversions. Nor would they have misinterpreted ghost contacts from unusual electromagnetic interference or signals from other radar. The air bases at Aachen and Maastricht were notified and an AWACS – airborne warning and control system – aircraft was sent to the area from its home base at Gelsenkirchen.

By that time the Flying Triangle had been seen by another nineteen gendarmes who had been attending a social event near Eupen. Other witnesses from Liége, Eupen, Plombiéres, Kittenis, Baelin, Verviers, Jalhay, St Vith, Andrimont, Lontzen, Voeren, Battice and Herbesthal, called the gendarmerie to report seeing a UFO. The descriptions from the witnesses tallied, and there was no doubt that they were all seeing the same object. The sightings cover a period of some two-and-half hours.

Some fifty-five minutes after the first sighting, the same two gendarmes saw another Flying Triangle – but this time it was much larger. It appeared almost at ground level from behind a small wood. It made a climbing turn while slowly rotating in a horizontal plane. Its speed was relatively slow, about forty miles an hour, and it followed the course of a nearby main road.

The first few sightings passed without reaction even though they were seen not just by gendarmes and the general public but also by trained observers from the Belgian military. These are not the type of people who are likely to confuse a conventional object with a UFO. However, in December 1989, the Royal Belgian Air Force was inundated by hundreds of calls from terrified citizens who had seen large triangular craft hovering at an altitude of around 350 feet. It had a light at each corner and gave off a 'light humming noise'.

Over the next few months the Belgian Air Force was scrambled several times, but the alien craft were to fast for even NATO's fastest aircraft. As a member of NATO, Belgium had a squadron of F-16 jet fighters permanently on standby. Throughout the Cold War, NATO jet fighters regularly had to see off Warsaw Pact planes probing Western defences. Soviet MiGs were easy to pick up on radar, but the Russians liked to show off the superiority of their aircraft in a deadly game to check NATO reaction times. But while the Belgian Air Force could handle themselves well enough against the Soviets, they were not up to handling aliens. The F-16 had a top speed of well over 1,250 miles an hour but, no matter how fast they scrambled, by the time they got aloft they were too late to find anything. Witnesses had seen the triangular craft make off at incredible speeds. Despite their lack of success, the Belgian air ministry were not about to dismiss the matter. It drew up plans to deal with future incursions into its airspace. Nothing, not even a UFO, was allowed to enter its Belgian jurisdiction without official clearance.

The next time a Belgian F-16 was sent aloft it found something. What people were reporting as a UFO was the light from a laser display. After that, the Belgian Air Force command decided that its fighters would only be scrambled if a visual sighting was matched by a radar contact or could be confirmed by the local police. On the night of 30 March 1990, and in the early hours of the following day, these new criteria were put to the test.

The preliminary sightings were focused on the Wavre region of central Belgium, around fourteen miles south-east of Brussels. At around 11 p.m., the phone of the Wavre gendarmerie began ringing. On the other end of the line was a witness who claimed to have seen a huge triangular UFO hovering in the night sky. The night sky was clear and the man said that the lights at the corners of the craft shone more brightly than the stars. There was no doubt in the witness's mind that what he was seeing was a UFO. A Wavre gendarme ran outside, then ran back to the phone to confirm the sighting. He noted that the UFO had the same massive triangular shape with the same lighting configuration as seen at Eupen four months earlier.

The police called the radar station at Glons near Tongeren in north-east Belgium for confirmation. Glons radar confirmed the sighting of an unidentified object at an altitude of ten thousand feet. The NATO radar station at Semmerzake confirmed the Glons finding and passed its confirmation onto the Belgian Air Force. The radar scans were compared with the previous Eupen radar sightings at Semmerzake and Glons and were found to be identical. By this time the phones were red hot. Worried witnesses were reporting sightings of three lights flying in a perfect triangular formation. Many people clearly saw that these lights were on the underside of a huge, triangular craft.

Colonel Wilfred de Brouwer, chief of the operations section of the Belgian Air Force, said, 'Because of the frequency of requests for radar confirmation at Glons and Semmerzake – and as a number of private visual observations had been confirmed by the police – it was decided that as these parameters had been met, a patrol of F-16 aircraft should be sent to intercept an unidentified object somewhere to the south of Brussels.'

As a result, two F-16 aircraft of the Belgian Air Force, flown by a captain and a flight lieutenant, both highly qualified pilots, took off from Bevekom. Guided by the radar station, the pilots soon located the object. Their on-board radar made contact at a height of two thousand feet. By this time, the UFO was hovering menacingly over the suburbs of Brussels. As the F-16s tore towards the intruder, they locked their weapons system on to it when they were still around seven miles away. From this point, any missile they fired would have hit the target – if the target was a conventional aircraft.

'I've got lock on,' reported one of the F-16 pilots. 'Repeat. I've got lock on. Approaching target now. Wait. Target beginning to move. Trying to follow. I've lost it. Repeat. I've lost it. Target has moved, target has moved. Attempting to lock on again. I have it. Closing in… closing… closing… It's gone. The target has gone.'

Then things got strange. Initially, the radar contact had been oval in shape. Suddenly, it changed to a diamond shape on their radar screens, and increased its speed instantly to 625 miles an hour. Over the next few minutes, the two F-16 pilots – who were among the most highly trained in NATO – managed to lock on to the target another six times. Three times they managed to lock on simultaneously. Each time, however, the craft simple shrugged them off by pursuing a violently erratic course at impossible speeds and losing its pursuers.

According to one of the pilots, the target was 'jumping around the radar screen like a dancing bee'. Two F-16s with locked-on missiles could have blown any known aircraft out of the sky, but in this case the pilots never got the chance to let loose a single warhead. Although its evasive action suggested that the craft was under intelligent control, the acceleration produced by the manoeuvres it made would have killed any living pilot. The photographic record of the on-board radar of the F-16s recorded a descent from 2,000 feet to 750 feet in two seconds, a rate of 1,125 miles an hour. The same photographs show an unbelievable acceleration rate of 175 miles to 1,125 miles an hour in a few seconds. According to Professor Leon Brenig, professor of physics at the Free University of Brussels, this would represent an acceleration of 46G – 46 times the force of gravity we experience on the surface of Earth – and way beyond the endurance of any human pilot. The maximum the human body can stand is around 8G. At the end of this descent the UFO came to an abrupt halt, which would have left any human pilot splattered over the instrument panel. Nevertheless, the craft moved off again as if nothing had happened. In spite of these incredible speeds and acceleration times, there were no sonic booms.

The movements of the UFO were described by the pilots and radar operators as 'wildly erratic and step-like' as it took a zigzag course over the city of Brussels with the two F-16s in pursuit. By this time, the pilots of the F-16s were alarmed. They realised that they were up against an infinitely superior craft and were, effectively, defenceless against it. But the UFO showed no hostile intentions. It dropped to just six hundred feet above a suburb of Brussels, then vanished from the radar as it disappeared into the lights of the city below. The pursuit had last over an hour.

'Immediately after the operation, the pilots said they had never seen anything like it,' said Colonel de Brouwer. 'Certainly the flight pattern and echo on their screens was in no way that of a conventional aircraft.'

Meanwhile, on the ground, all hell broke loose. Every military base, police station, TV and radio station saw its switchboard light up as some three thousand eyewitnesses from Eupen, Wavre, Liége and Brussels called in to report what they had seen – amazing if you consider that in the UK an average of two hundred eyewitnesses report UFOs a year. Over 2,600 statements were made to the police and the flight of the amazing craft had been captured on film and video. The whole country was in panic.

The Rodberg family had managed to film the craft from a distance of two hundred feet. One of the videos of the Flying Triangle came from Professor Brenig himself, who had observed the UFO through binoculars.

'It was like a triangular platform,' he said, 'with three very large lights on the base. There was also a smaller light in the middle. This was red and pulsating, while the other lights were yellow-white in colour. The thing flew slowly from north to south then, when it was almost overhead, rotated horizontally, spinning on its centre. Then it started to fly perpendicular to its original course.'

It was this rotation that convinced Professor Brenig he was seeing a UFO. 'The object did not incline like a normal aircraft,' he said. 'It was an unconventional shape and moved in an unconventional way.'

The Royal Belgian Air Force sent up more F-16s to search for the intruder. Belgium has around seventy F-16s in service and the skies were abuzz with activity. But despite this flurry of activity, the Belgian Air Force realised it had one big problem. What was it going to do if one of its planes located the elusive UFO?

Later, the Belgian Air Force was quizzed about the events of 30 March 1990 and co-operated with a Belgian UFO research group carrying out a detailed investigation. Attempts were made to find some rational, or at least comforting, explanation for what occurred that night. The standard explanation for a UFO sighting is that it is a weather balloon, especially when it is seen to hang in the air. But weather balloons are usually round, not triangular, and no weather balloon has ever pulled 46G in a dive.

Another standard explanation for UFO sightings is that they are secret tests of military aircraft. But the Belgian government is not in the business of developing new aircraft, and a quick check of the air ministry's records revealed that no foreign government had requested permission to make test flights over Belgium on that date. Why would anyone test a top-secret military aircraft on a clear night over a well-populated city rather than in some deserted area, anyway?

Claims that the Flying Triangles must have been the US testing a new type of Stealth aircraft are disproved by the fact that the UFO appeared on both ground-based and airborne radar. The whole point of Stealth planes is that they are invisible to radar. The amazing manoeuvres of the Belgian Flying Triangle could not be explained as a holographic projection on the clouds. On the night of 30 March 1990 the sky over Belgium was entirely free of cloud – that is why some three thousand people saw the UFOs.

The Belgian Air Force chief of staff went on record to express the military's consternation.

'The Air Force has arrived at the conclusion that a number of anomalous phenomena have been produced within Belgian air space,' he said. And he conceded that the UFO that had penetrated Belgian air space without authority on 30 March 1990 was a solid, structured craft.

Major Lambrechts of the Royal Belgian Air Force prepared an official report that reveled just how seriously the Belgian authorities took the matter.

'Since early September 1989,' it said, 'strange phenomena were regularly witnessed in Belgian air space.' It went on to dismiss some of the possible explanations that had been offered. 'The presence of and/or tests with B2 or F-117A [Stealth planes], remotely piloted vehicles… and AWACS at the time of the happenings can be excluded.'

The lights on the UFOs, Lambrechts reported, 'were very clear, as if they were signals; this enables [us] to distinguish them from the stars.' The report also admited that 'contact was observed by different sensors [radar] of the Air Force' and concluded: 'This report is based on eyewitness accounts by police officers on duty whose objectivity and common sense is beyond doubt.'

Colonel de Brouwer, Air Force chief of operations that night, concluded: 'Even if until now there has been no threat, one must accept the fact that for the past six months the Belgian skies have experienced extraordinary phenomena.' And the Belgian Minister of Defence said in parliament that 'the government did not know what they were'.

This is quite an admission in view of the fact that officialdom the world over routinely denies the existence of UFOs.

The Triangle Returns

Three years later, the Flying Triangle put in an appearance over the UK. Most of the sightings occurred in the early hours of 31 March 1993. Nick Pope, who manned the desk at the Ministry of Defence that handles UFO sightings, recalled: 'Calls came in all morning from people, many of them police officers, saying they had seen these huge triangular craft.'

The descriptions were similar to the Belgian and Hudson Valley sightings. Many witnesses reported three lights moving in perfect formation. Others who had been closer said that the lights simply marked the corners of a huge, triangular craft. Witnesses also reported that the craft gave off a deep humming sound. A family in Staffordshire in the Midlands reported seeing a UFO hovering over their house. Again it made a low humming noise.

Along with reports from the police came sightings by military personnel guarding bases. One came from RAF Cosford in Shropshire. There, an entire military guard patrol reported seeing the UFO pass directly over the base. They checked with duty air traffic controllers, but drew a complete blank. According to the logs, there were no aircraft in the area.

Having heard about the UFO sighting at Cosford, the meteorological officer at RAF Shawbury, only a few miles away, went outside to see if he could see anything. What he saw was a triangular craft flying directly towards the base. It was emitting a low humming sound. He estimated the size of the object as being only a little smaller than a 747. Others said it was the size of a Hercules transport plane – but neither jumbo jets nor Hercules can hover. Shawbury's met officer reported that the UFO came to a halt and shone a beam of light on the ground. The beam swept from side to side, as if the craft was looking for something. Then the light went out and the UFO passed slowly over the base, almost directly overhead.

The Ministry of Defence launched a full investigation. Officially the MoD has always maintained that UFO sightings were 'of no defence significance', so it needed to discover a mundane explanation for the sightings. The problem here was that a number of their own personnel had reported seeing an unidentified triangular craft flying, unhampered, directly over two key military establishments.

At least ninety per cent of UFO sightings have a conventional explanation, so the MoD began checking on aircraft activity, airship flights and weather balloon launches. Again, it found nothing in the area at the time. So it then checked with the Royal Observatory to see if there might be an astronomical explanation, such as unusual meteorite activity. The observatory reported that a Russian rocket had re-entered the Earth's atmosphere. This had been responsible for the appearance of strange lights at high altitude for a few minutes at around 1.10 a.m. But the UFO the RAF personnel had seen was low down and the sightings happened over a period of several hours. The sightings at Cosford and Shawbury could not be explained by the rocket's re-entry and this theory was discounted.

Again, the theory that the Flying Triangle might be some sort of secret, prototype craft was investigated. For years, there had been rumours of a hypersonic replacement for the Lockheed SR-71 Blackbird, called Aurora. The Belgian Air Force had investigated similar possibilities, but both the Belgian and British authorities were given categorical assurances by the American government that no US aircraft were involved. Besides, it is hardly likely that a secret aircraft would be tested in heavily defended air space without proper diplomatic clearance. The MoD had no choice but to reject the theory that the UFO was an American prototype aircraft. 'Flying Triangle clearly behaves in a way that is beyond the cutting edge of our technology,' said MoD UFOlogist Nick Pope. So, like the Belgian government before it, the British government were forced to admit that they could find no explanation.

However, there is one interesting connection between the sightings in Belgium and the UK. Both occurred late at night on 30 March, and in the early hours of the next day. If these UFO stories were reported in the media, the stories would have appeared on 1 April – April Fool's Day? Is this just a coincidence? Or does it point to an elaborate hoax? Or perhaps, the aliens who built and fly the craft have a sense of humour.

But this is no laughing matter. In both Belgium and the UK, the UFOs were observed by military personnel. From their observations it is clear that NATO could do nothing to stop the uninvited intruders. And, whatever the authorities say, that has national security implications.

RAF Cosford

This is not the first time RAF Cosford has played host to a UFO. On 10 December 1963, two RAF personnel saw a strange domed object sweeping the airfield there with a strange green beam. As they ran to get help, it crashed behind a hanger. When they returned, it was nowhere to be seen.

The two men were then subjected to a rigorous interrogation, but their story could not be shaken. However, a couple of days later, a very large transport plane landed. This was an extremely unusual event at Cosford. A large object hidden under tarpaulins was loaded up and flown off.

Mexican Sightings

Sceptics often ask why UFOs and aliens always appear to lonely people in the back of beyond. But that is not true. On the afternoon of 11 July 1991, a UFO appeared over the world's most populous metropolis, Mexico City, where it was seen by millions of people. And it did not turn up on just any old day. It appeared on a day and at a time when the inhabitants of Mexico's capital would inevitably be turning their attention to the skies. It was the day of an eclipse of the sun, which would turn day into night in Mexico City for over six minutes. Spectacular though the eclipse was, it was upstaged by an extraterrestrial craft that managed to steal the attention of tens

The ancient Mayan prophecy that the Masters of the Stars would return at the birth of the sixth Sun, heralding a new age of cosmic awareness, was fulfilled on 11 July 1991 when many UFOs were seen and filmed.

of thousands of spectators.

At 1:22 p.m., just as the eclipse was starting, a shiny metallic object appeared in the sky. It hovered silently near the eclipsing sun, floating there for a half an hour. In that time, not only thousands saw it, but at least seventeen different people in various locations around the city had filmed it on video. For the next few months, Mexico was in the grip of 'UFO fever'. One of those caught up in it was one of country's most respected TV journalists and host to the popular news programme *60 Minutos*, Jaime Maussan. Previously Maussan had had no interest in UFOs.

'I am a journalist and, as such, I only wish to deal with the facts,' he said. 'However, since I became involved with this, along with the rest of Mexico, I have seen overwhelming evidence which convinces me that my country is being visited regularly by a huge number of extraterrestrial craft. There is no other explanation.'

Soon after the eclipse, Maussan made an appeal on TV, asking the public to send in any footage they had shot of the UFO. There was an overwhelming response. The TV company was inundated with spectacular video footage which showed the unidentified craft spinning on its own axis. But it did not stop there.

'Since the eclipse, there has been a UFO flap – people, almost daily, are witnessing the most intense manifestation of the UFO phenomenon,' said Mexican UFO researcher Santiago Yturria Gorza. And the public continued to send in videotapes of UFOs spotted since the eclipse.

On the day of the eclipse, a UFO also appeared over the town of

Puebla. A disc-shaped craft was filmed moving slowly and silently through the sky. It was seen by thousands of Mexicans who had lined the streets to watch the eclipse. A UFO had also been filmed in the area four days before. Then in January 1996, streaks of light appeared in the night sky over Puebla. These were seen by dozens of witnesses. Examining film taken of them, astronomers initially dismissed them as comets, but later analysis showed that they were too low and too slow to be comets.

On 5 May 1994, a pulsating craft in the sky above the district of Juarez in Chihuahua was filmed separately by two neighbours, Senora Rosi Uribe and Francisco Javier. Known to UFOlogists as the 'plasma ship' because of its internal pulsating light, similar craft have been seen over Mexico on numerous occasions since 1991. Carlos Dias, a professional photographer, had photographed them regularly. One even put in an appearance on Mexico's Independence Day in 1991, seemingly observing a Mexican air force fly-by. It turned up again in 1993, passing through a helicopter formation.

In collaboration with American husband-and-wife private-detective team Lee and Brit Elders, Maussan produced a series of three remarkable documentaries called *The Messengers of Destiny.* These have been widely acclaimed throughout the UFO community for showing some of the best UFO footage ever shot. In the eyes of UFOlogists, the video evidence collected by Maussan demonstrates that, whatever UFOs are, they are not the product of any technology known to humans. One video showed a UFO flying through cloud. Sceptics say that the object could be a plane, a meteorite, or even a bird. But computer analysis of the sequence clearly demonstrated that it was a solid, metallic, disc-shaped craft. Computer enhancement of the image also revealed two other, smaller craft flying just below the main structure that were otherwise invisible to the naked eye.

Dozens of videos showed a single UFO that slowly split into two separate craft. On one tape, a UFO could be seen splitting into five distinct entities. Computer analysis also revealed the incredible manoeuvrability of these craft. They were seen accelerating at rates that would kill any human pilot and moving at seemingly impossible speed across the sky. One UFO zoomed out of sight in the space of a single video frame – it had disappeared from a clear sky in under a sixtieth of a second.

The Mexican sightings have provided a huge amount of solid evidence to support the idea that UFOs are extraterrestrial in origin. The video footage went way beyond the fleeting glimpses of UFOs seen before, and analysis of their aerial activity confounds any terrestrial explanation. The regular explanations of UFO sightings – that they are the planet Venus, weather balloons or meteorites – could easily be dismissed in this case, and UFO sceptics have studiously avoided studying Maussan's video material.

With the Mexican evidence for the presence of UFOs unrefuted, the question remains: why had the aliens chosen the skies above Mexico City to reveal themselves? Jaime Maussan believes that its inhabitants have been chosen to test human reactions towards the arrival of extraterrestrials. He thinks the aliens are being so open about their presence that this must herald something else.

Other researchers point out that more than a thousand years ago the Maya, who occupied southern Mexico before the Spanish conquest, predicted the birth of the 'sixth sun' in the period following the eclipse of the sun in 1991. Then the 'Masters of the Stars' or the 'Messengers of Destiny' would return. The Mayans were accomplished astronomers and could calculate eclipses with extraordinary accuracy. According to the Dresden Codex, a stone table that depicts Mayan cosmology: 'In the era of the sixth sun, all that is buried will be discovered, truth shall be the seed of light and the sons of the sixth sun shall be the ones who travel through the stars.'

Although their purpose has yet to be revealed, the strange objects in the skies above Mexico continue to be seen and videoed. Subsequent footage showed UFO fleets of several craft flying in a formation that resembled the constellations. This may be an attempt at communication. However, there may be a more sinister interpretation. In 1995, security camera tapes from Nellis Air Force Base in Nevada, home of America's secret research establishment Area 51, fell into the hands of UFO researchers. They showed a pulsating metallic craft climbing through the sky. When compared to Maussan's footage by researchers from the US TV programme *Sightings* the following year they proved to be identical.

The Nellis footage has been authenticated by a handful of American defence analysts, including leading Stealth-technology researcher Bill Sweetman. Could it be that the US military are testing a secret weapons programme in Mexican air space?

Encounters at Gulf Breeze

The small holiday resort of Gulf Breeze, which lies on a peninsula in north-west Florida, has fewer than ten thousand residents. Otherwise unexceptionable, in the late 1980s it became one of the great hotspots of UFO activity. The sightings began on 11 November 1987, when building contractor Ed Walters claims to have seen and filmed one of the most dramatic UFO encounters ever to be recorded. Although Gulf Breeze has since become a Mecca for UFOlogists and numerous other sightings have been

Display of UFO photographs from Gulf Breeze, Florida, at the 1988 Mutual UFO Network (MUFON) Symposium.

made there, the Walters' case remains the best documented. Walters claims to have a ninety-eight-second videotape of his UFO encounter, along with some forty genuine photographs of the craft. More sinisterly, he also claims that the UFO tried to abduct him.

Walters' first encounter took place on the afternoon of 11 November. He was working at home, when his attention was drawn to a strange light outside. It appeared to be coming from behind a thirty-foot pine tree in his front yard. The glowing object was partially obscured by the tree, so Walters left his home office to investigate. But when he opened the front door, he saw, a large, glowing, bluish-grey craft floating silently above the ground. With amazing presence of mind, Walters ducked back inside the house, grabbed his Polaroid camera and started snapping.

The excitement made him foolhardy and Walters rushed outside to get a better view. The extraterrestrial craft, which was now directly above him, emitted a pulsing beam of blue light from its underside.

'I stared at the object hovering over my front yard then… Bang! Something hit me all over my body,' he said. An energy beam paralysed Walters, lifted him three feet in the air and held him there for around twenty seconds.

'I tried to lift my arms to point the camera,' he said. 'I couldn't move them. I was in a blue light beam. Then my feet lifted off the ground and as I began to scream a deep computer-like voice groaned in my head, "We will not harm you." But it was in my head, not in my ears.'

Walters also managed to capture the blue beam descending from the glowing underside of the portholed, disc-shaped craft on film.

Initially, Walters sent the photographs anonymously to his local paper, *The Sentinel*. When they published them, a number of other witnesses contacted the paper. They reported seeing a similar craft at around the same time and their descriptions matched his photographs.

Walters continued seeing strange silent objects hovering in the sky, backing his claims with more photographs and video footage.

On 12 January 1988, he photographed the alien craft hovering over his truck. Five 'beings' from it landed on the road in front of him, but he did not manage to photograph them. Walters has no idea why the aliens are visiting him.

'I don't even know if these "beings" are alien,' he said. 'I have not idea what they are.'

The wave of sightings in Gulf Breeze attracted national attention and the small town became the centre of a media circus. Then MUFON – the Mutual UFO Network, a grassroots organisation of private citizens who have taken it upon themselves to get to the bottom of the UFO phenomena – turned up. Key to their investigation was the authenticity of the Walters' photographs and video footage. Several experts were called in. The most prominent among them was the optical physicist Dr Bruce Maccabee. A former US government researcher, he is widely respected among the UFO community for his unbiased scientific approach. Maccabee began by inspecting the site of the encounters. Then he conducted a series of detailed, personal interviews with all the witnesses. The photographs were analysed using state-of-the-art computer equipment. At the end of his rigorous investigation, Maccabee could find no evidence of a hoax. The photographs, he said, were authentic images of 'unconventional aircraft'. But the video footage proved harder to authenticate.

'With enough time, money, luck and skill – anything can be faked,' says MUFON's video analyst Jeff Soinio.

However, the Gulf Breeze sightings also attracted the attention of the sceptics. Philip Klass, author and well-known UFO debunker, claimed that Walters' photographs were clever double exposures. He said that models had been photographed under clever lighting conditions, then combined with photographs of the sky to provide the background. A model bearing a remarkable similarity to detailed sketches Walters made of the craft he saw was found in the attic of his previous home. He claims that it had been planted to discredit him.

To rebut Klass's allegations, MUFON gave Walters a sealed four-lens stereo camera, which is practically tamper-proof. The new pictures Walters took with this camera, UFO enthusiasts claim, provided conclusive proof of his sightings. But the sceptics were still not convinced. Among them, surprisingly, was Barbara Becker, a MUFON member herself and keen amateur photographer of twenty years, standing. The photographs may be genuine, she conceded, but the UFOs themselves she claimed were ingenious fakes.

'The fact that Walters took more than forty excellent photographs is enough to arouse suspicions,' she said. 'Ed loves to tell a good story – so much so, that he couldn't restrain himself from embellishing his accounts of the incidents in his books.'

In fact, Walters has written three books about his encounters. One, called *UFOs Are Real: Here's The Proof*, was co-authored with Dr Bruce Maccabee.

However, Barbara Becker's position was soon contradicted by a flurry of new sightings. In the following six months, more than a hundred witnesses reported other UFO sightings in the Gulf Breeze area, and they produced more photographs and video footage to back their claims. To most people, this vindicated Walters. However, some of the die-hard sceptics investigating the case claimed that the entire population of Gulf Breeze was involved in the hoax.

The inhabitants of Gulf Breeze took being called liars amiss, so, with the residents of nearby Pensacola, they organised surveillance teams to monitor the air space of western Florida day and night, calling themselves the Skywatchers. In a matter of weeks, they saw a bright red and amber light zigzagging across the sky, before it finally disappeared. Several more UFO sightings followed. Usually these involved small points of light in the sky that changed size rapidly, moved at odd angles, travelled at unimaginable speeds and accelerated at rates thought to be impossible, all without making a sound. However, these new sightings were hard to substantiate. In the immediate area of Gulf Breeze, there were three major military bases, all of which generated extensive air traffic. MUFON investigator Gary Watson said that the military was always asked whether aircraft were in the air when the

Skywatchers made a sighting. On each occasion, they confirmed that no aircraft were aloft at the time.

In 1991, Gulf Breeze MUFON president Art Hufford photographed an unexplained source of light in the night sky, which suddenly disappeared after ten seconds. It was witnessed by over thirty people. One of the luckiest UFO watchers in the area was photographer Bland Pugh. In 1991, he captured two UFOs in one shot. One orange-coloured UFO left an extraordinary corkscrew trail across the sky, while seeming to drop a white UFO from its belly. Nicknamed 'Bubba', the object has been seen by residents a number of times and MUFON member Bruce Morrison managed to capture this particular event on video.

Then in 1993, Pugh photographed what looked like a white light in the sky. But when it was enhanced, a black craft appeared above it. And in 1996, Pugh snapped a pulsating orange 'doughnut', similar to the glowing ring Walters said he saw on the underside of the UFO that visited him in 1987.

It has become increasingly hard for debunkers to deny that something odd is going on in the skies above Gulf Breeze, though sceptics remain convinced that Walters is a publicity-seeking con man. Meanwhile, the UFO community point to the overwhelming evidence Walters has presented and the fact that for years after the Ed Walters story broke the sightings continued.

'There will always be people who choose not to believe, whatever the evidence suggests,' said Walters. 'Some simply refuse to accept that UFOs exist, so ultimately they brand me a hoaxer.'

Rendezvous Français

On the afternoon of 8 January 1981, Renato Nicolai – an Italian living in Trans-en-Provence, a small village in the south of France – was building a concrete shelter for the water pump he had recently installed behind his house. Renato had hoped to finish the work before nightfall, but at 5 p.m. he heard a strange noise coming from above. As he looked up he noticed a strange object descending onto a nearby hill.

'I was startled by a light whistling,' he said. 'The noise was unusual, so I turned round and lifted my head. Above the tall pine tree at the bottom of my land I saw a craft descending towards the ground without rotating.'

The object he described was small, only a few feet in diameter, like 'two bowls turned one on of top of the other'. It was metallic grey in colour and had small 'landing' legs on its base. It was some two hundred feet away.

Intrigued, Renato walked over to it to take a closer look. He assumed that it was a military craft in distress – there was an air base not far away at Canjuers – and the craft looked more like it was falling than making a controlled descent.

The UFO hit the ground with a thud. Discretion being the better part of valour, Renato stopped behind a hut next to the small field where the UFO had come to rest. From there, he was just thirty yards from the craft with a clear field of vision.

'It stood on some sort of small feet and measured 1.8 metres in height by about 2.5 metres in diameter,' he said. 'In the centre, there was a kind of metal crown separating the two bowls.'

The craft sat there, inert.

'There were no flames or smoke,' he said. 'There wasn't even any light.'

After a couple of minutes, Renato came out from behind the hut and walked over towards the craft. But as he approached the object it suddenly started to make a very high-pitched whistling noise, then shot away vertically at an amazing speed.

Renato followed the path of the UFO with his eyes, as its strange whistling sound resonated in his ears. As the UFO shot skywards, he could see an opening underneath the craft, but he saw no flames or smoke came out of it. Renato recalled something else strange about the craft.

'As it left the ground,' he said, 'it picked up a small amount of earth.'

Once the UFO had disappeared behind the trees, Renato approached the landing site and he saw clear marks on the ground where it had stood. That evening, when his wife came home, he told her what he'd seen. She did not believe him so, the following morning, he took her out into the field and showed her the marks on the ground. She phoned neighbours, who came round to have a look. Then they notified the police.

On Friday, 9 January 1981, the Draguignan gendarmerie received a call reporting a UFO sighting. They went to investigate. When the gendarmes reached the site, they examined the marks. According to their notes, these consisted of two concentric circles, one 2.4 metres in diameter and the other 2.2 metres inside it. The edges showed evidence of scraping, as if whatever made them had been skidding or spinning on its axis. Another mark could be seen on a low wall near by. The object had plainly crashed into the wall before skidding to a halt in the field.

The gendarmes then took the witness's statement and collected a number of samples of plants and soil from the site. These samples were sent for analysis in Toulouse. The police then announced that they could find no logical explanation for the sightings and handed over the case to the government agency responsible for dealing with UFO cases.

At that time, the agency charged with investigating unidentified aerial phenomenon in France was the *Groupe d'Etude des Phénoménes Aérospatioux Non-identifiés* (GEPAN). This group was more than capable of investigating such a case. It had the expertise of a number of scientific experts – physicists, biologists and psychologists – to call on. However, the police report on the incident arrived at GEPAN headquarters on Monday, 12 January, but their investigators did not turn up at Trans-en-Provence for over a month. By then, the evidence in Renato's field had disappeared.

However, GEPAN could not overlook the samples that the police had sent to various labs, or the detailed measurements the gendarmes had made of the marks at the site. Eventually GEPAN had to release a highly censored technical report – though the names of all the people, places and laboratories involved were deliberately removed. The report stated that the gendarmes' description of the marks left in Renato Nicolai's field showed the earth had been crushed. A very heavy object had stood at the site.

The soil samples showed that the ground had been heated to a temperature of between 300 and 600°C. Various materials had been deposited at the site, principally iron and phosphates along with residues from the combustion process. Unusually high levels of zinc were also found. And the plants in the area were found to have been bleached of fifty per cent of their chlorophyll. The vegetation samples passed on to professor of biochemistry Michel Bounias showed signs of senescence, a biochemical ageing of the leaves that can only be explained as a result of artificial processes.

'One thing's for certain: we know nothing of the nature or the origin of the phenomenon,' said biochemist Michel Bounias. 'And this is where the real problem starts, because I've never come across anything like it on the planet.'

Renato was interviewed by psychologists who concluded that he was telling the truth and he had hard evidence to corroborate his story. But still GEPAN investigators tried to find some logical explanation for the sighting: helicopters, weather balloons, stray shells. So far they have come up with nothing that can explain what happened on 8 January 1981 in Trans-en-Provence. Meanwhile, Jean-Pierre Petit, head of the French Centre for Scientific Research, offered his expert opinion on the case:

'In order to back the "case for UFOs" with something of real consequence, you need to produce hard evidence that cannot easily be reproduced by humans,' he says. 'The Trans-en-Provence case offers this kind of objective proof, which, in this instance, comes in the form of a significant alteration in the environment.

'Biochemists agree that the pigmentary structure of the plants is not only stable, but also difficult to modify. Moreover, Michel Bounias carried out a parallel study on the samples in order to quantify the radioactive source that had affected them. The results suggested gamma rays as high as one megarad in intensity, a level of exposure capable of killing all bacterial life and sterilising food stuffs.

'Radioactivity specialists will tell you that, given the area affected, exposure to such a high level of gamma radiation for thirty seconds represents a significant quantity of energy. So this is not exactly the work of a DIY enthusiast. Even if the Atomic Energy Commission had wanted to pull such a stunt, it wouldn't exactly have been a piece of cake.

'In this case... the hypothesis of some kind of vehicle must be considered, simply because it is the most plausible. Were the "case for UFOs" subject to a judicial inquiry, the investigating magistrate would be forced to admit the Trans-en-Provence incident as evidence.'

The Amaranth Case

Another remarkably similar case occurred the following year in France. On 21 October 1982, an egg-shaped UFO was seen flying over a French garden. It came to a halt and hovered over an amaranth bush for twenty minutes, before shooting skywards. It was seen by a prominent metallurgist, who managed to get within two feet of it and, at one point, managed to touch it. He said that the craft was about 80 centimetres in height and 1.5 m in diameter. The upper half was marine blue, the lower half gun-metal grey.

Once it had gone, the bush was left a dark brown colour. Its centre had been dehydrated. The seeds had ripened spontaneously and some of their heads had burst. Again GEPAN was called in to investigate.

'The fact that the leaves had dried out and the husks of certain fruits had burst could have been due to the corona effect of an electric field,' said their report.

As in the Trans-en-Provence case, Michel Bounias concluded that: 'It would be useful to compare our observations with the effects of other physical agents, such as electromagnetic field generators.'

Down Under

The Knowles family were driving across the great limestone plateau of the Nullarbor Plain in southern Australia on the night of 20 January 1988, when they experienced one of the southern hemisphere's most famous UFO encounters. The Knowleses were travelling from Perth to Melbourne to visit family. Sean Knowles was driving. Also in the car were his mother Faye Knowles, his two younger brothers, Patrick and Wayne, and the family's two dogs.

At about 1:30 a.m. they were heading east along the Eyre Highway towards Mundrabilla, when the car radio began picking up strange interference. Then it packed up. Some ten or fifteen minutes later, Sean saw something on the road ahead of him. At first he thought it was a truck with only one headlight. As it approached, he could see it was indeed a truck. But the light he'd seen was not a single headlight. It came from a strange glowing ball that hovered above the vehicle. What's more, the truck was driving erratically down the wrong side of the road. Sean swerved to avoid a collision, narrowly missing the wayward truck.

A little later, the Sean saw a car with a similar ball of light hovering above it. Sean was determined to find out what was going on. He turned around and began to follow the car and its glowing companion. The he woke up Patrick who was asleep in the front passenger seat beside him.

'Look at that Pat,' he said. 'There's something in front of us. I think it's a UFO.'

As they approached it, they saw it was now hovering over an old station wagon. And it was coming at them. They swerved to avoid it, ending up on the other side of the road. Then the ball of light doubled back again and started following them. Quickly Sean turned around again and made off. By this time, everyone in the car was in a desperate panic. Faye and the children were screaming, but it was too late. They could not outrun it. The glowing object quickly caught up with them and landed on the roof of the car with a loud bang.

'The next thing we knew, the object was on the roof and had picked the car up off the ground,' said Patrick.

Bright beams of light bathed the car's interior. The dogs went crazy and everyone thought they were going to die. Patrick said he felt as if his brains were being sucked out of his head. Sean was still trying to escape the light. He had not noticed was that the car was not on the ground at all. Under the influence of the UFO, it had been drawn up into the air. With his foot flat to the floor, Sean estimated that his speed was over 125 miles an hour.

In a state of panic, Faye, who was in the back, wound down her window. She reached up out of the window and touched the object. It felt warm and spongy, like some form of suction pad, she said. The sensation made her recoil violently. Pulling her hand back in, she found it was red, swollen and cold. Seeing this, she began to scream and became hysterical.

Patrick rolled the front window down. The inside of the car was suddenly covered with a black, ash-like substance that smelt of 'decomposing bodies'. Everyone's hair stood on end and their voices became distorted, as if everything was happening in slow motion. Suddenly the alien craft released them. The car dropped back onto the road, bursting one of the rear tyres. It was only then that Sean realised that the car had been flying through the air.

He now jammed on the brakes. When the car came to a stop, the family got out and ran for cover. They hid in some nearby bushes. The UFO was still in the vicinity. It hovered above, shining a searchlight down on to the ground as if it was searching for them, while they watched, petrified, from the undergrowth. The object, they said, resembled 'an egg in a cup' and emitted a low humming sound. The craft kept circling the area but, when the sun began to come up, it vanished.

Sean changed the tyre and, for about a quarter of an hour, their voices remained strangely distorted. Things were just getting back to normal when they saw that the UFO was coming back. The family jumped in the car and Sean hurtled off in the direction of the Mundrabilla Roadhouse, which was about twenty-five miles away. On the way, they hit a kangaroo, which dented the wing, but the car stayed on the road. They continued at a frantic pace and it was only when they were in sight of the service station that the UFO stopped following them and mysteriously disappeared again.

When they arrived at the Mundrabilla Roadhouse, the family told two truck drivers what had happened.

'I thought at first they were trying to be funny when they were telling me about their experience,' said the service station attendant. 'They were excited and scared. When I got near the car, I noticed an odour similar to that of hot insulation.' He also noticed that the family were visibly shaken. Faye's hand was still badly swollen and the dogs had started to lose hair in clumps.

The Knowles encounter was investigated by Paul Norman of the Victorian UFO Research Society (VUFORS). He caught up with Knowleses ten days later, on 30 January, in Adelaide and began his investigation by inspecting their car. He found that the radio that had malfunctioned during the encounter was now working fine. However, marks on the roof correlated with the family's account of what had happened.

During the encounter, Sean had said that he had been driving at over 125 miles an hour. According to the manufacturers, the model of Ford Telstra the Knowleses were driving was incapable of such a speed. However, in a TV documentary on the encounter by Australia's Channel Seven, the car was tested with its front wheels off the floor and it was shown that the car could, in fact, reach such speeds.

The dust that had covered the inside of the car during the encounter was tested in Adelaide and was found to be mostly iron oxide, which is often produced by worn brake pads. But one of the truck drivers the family had talked to at the Mundrabilla Roadhouse, a Mr Henly, was also a keen racing driver. He said that the dust looked like silicon. It had an incredible feel to it, and it was nothing like brake dust. And the first police officer to arrive after the incident also said that the dust he found in the Knowleses' car was not from the brakes.

To check this out further, Norman sent a sample to a NASA lab in California. Their analysis showed that it was made up mainly of silicon, carbon, oxygen and potassium and could not have come from the brake pads. The sample also carried a trace of astatine – a radioactive chemical that can only be produced synthetically. Its half-life is only a few hours, so even a large amount should have disappeared long before the investigation got under way. Nevertheless the radiation was there and would help to explain Faye's swollen hand.

Norman also investigated the blown-out tyre. Normally, when a tyre blows out at the speed the Knowleses were travelling, it would have split apart like a peeled mandarin. But the Knowles tyre had blown in a very unusual way – it had ripped all the way around the circumference.

Despite all the evidence to the contrary, the Nullarbor case has generally been dismissed as a hoax. Philip Klass, the America's most famous UFO debunker, claims that marks on the car's roof were actually caused by a roof rack. The Knowleses say that no roof rack had ever been attached to their vehicle. Klass also says that the UFO encounter had been invented for insurance purposes, that Sean Knowles fell asleep at the wheel and came off the road, hence the damaged tyre. The Knowleses vehemently deny this. Other sceptics say that the family saw a meteorite or, more preposterously, the sun rising. Other 'scientific' explanations include that they encountered a stray missile from Woomera Test Range in the Great Victoria Desert, that they were gripped by an unusual form of electrically charged tornado or that they were suffering a collective hallucination caused by driving for long hours in the desert at night.

However, a dispassionate evaluation of the evidence suggests that something mysterious did happen on the Nullarbor Plain that night, and the case still intrigues members of the UFO community around the world. Certainly for the Knowles it was a very real experience.

Wide Load

Gary Wood was driving home from work with his friend Colin down a motorway in Scotland one night around 10:30 p.m. As they were going around a corner, Colin pointed out of the windscreen at something hovering above the road. They were about a hundred yards from it.

'As we got closer, I could see the object in great detail,' said Gary. 'It was a black, circular object, about thirty-five feet wide, and was in three parts, with pieces hanging underneath.'

They began to panic. Gary was too scared to stop the car, but jammed it into second gear and accelerated hard underneath it. Colin was shouting and screaming. Just as they headed under the object, a curtain of light descended. Suddenly Gary found he was plunged into complete blackness. He was looking about for Colin but could see nothing. He tried to grab the car door, but it was not there. He had the sensation that he was not in his car any longer and thought he must have died. Then, suddenly, he was back in his car as it dropped back onto the road, damaging the bottom of the car. It ended up on an embankment. Later he discovered that he was missing two hours and, although the car was just one year old, it inexplicably began to rot away.

The Bonnybridge Triangle

Some places seem to attract more UFO sightings that others. These are so-called 'window areas'. One such is the area around Bonnybridge. It is so popular among UFOlogists that the Comfort Inn in Falkirk, in the middle of the so-called 'Bonnybridge Triangle', stages official UFO weekends. These have proved a great success, even attracting enthusiasts from the US and Japan. They come hoping to catch a glimpse of the strange lights in the sky that are seen and filmed regularly in the vicinity.

The idea of the Bonnybridge window began in 26 September 1992, when the newspaper *The Scotsman* carried an article written by Albert Morris. It was headlined 'Where on earth did the Martians go?' and its intention was to show that UFO sightings were falling. However, by accident, it drew attention to the fact that Scotland had two of the UK's five most prominent 'window areas'. The result was a media circus.

The other newspapers picked up on it, along with radio and TV. The *Glasgow Herald* claimed that 'Scotland was the top hotspot for UFOs', while the *Aberdeen Press* said that the skies above Scotland were teeming with aliens.

Into this furore stepped Malcolm McDonald, the Falkirk district environmental health officer. He had met a prominent local businessman who claimed to have had an encounter with a UFO. The council set up an investigation, in the course of which it became clear that the small Scottish town of Bonnybridge was the centre of a spate of encounters that had started the previous spring. The council's conclusions were published in the local press that November, and Bonnybridge took its place as a major new UFO hotspot. Council member Billy Buchanan was appointed UFO officer and, encouraged by the newspaper publicity, eyewitnesses began beating a path to his door.

Buchanan discovered that a wave of sightings had begun in March 1992, when a huge blue light, making a whirring and rattling sound, came out of some roadside trees, scaring three people who were walking down a back road to Bonnybridge. Buchanan called for more witnesses and, within a week, twenty-two cases were on record. Councillor Buchanan announced gravely that 'too many people have sighted UFOs for it to be dismissed lightly'. According to the *Glasgow Mail*, 'terrified townsfolk [were] scouring the sky at night, seeking UFOs'. Something had to be done. So Buchanan called in local UFO expert Malcolm Robinson to handle the situation. The media were soon calling Bonnybridge 'the UFO capital of the world', while Buchanan and Robinson set up a UFO hotline.

Sceptics point out that a plaque to commemorate a local UFO sighting erected in nearby Livingston had become something of a tourist attraction. While nobody was accusing the inhabitants of Bonnybridge of making up their sightings, many UFOlogists felt that the town council was skilfully manipulating the media attention the sightings had brought.

However, Malcolm Robinson went on record to say that many of the cases that had been reported were valuable and that something significant was really going on in Bonnybridge. Councillor Buchanan was singled out for praise. He responded like a true politician, organising open meetings in the town hall and sending letters to the Prime Minister, demanding government action to bring the truth about the Bonnybridge UFOs to light.

UFO Alley

However, Bonnybridge is far from being the UK's premier window area. Although it topped the sightings table in the early 1990s, there were few UFO encounters in the area before that time, and study a of fifty years' sighting statistics carried out for a TV documentary showed that, over the long term, UK UFO activity centred on a small area of northern England. The analysis found that around one tenth of all encounters in the UK occurred in a narrow, moorland region in the Pennine hills. The majority happened in a triangle that fell between the outer suburbs of the cities of Sheffield, Leeds and Manchester. It was found that the area that the local press had dubbed 'UFO alley' was a corridor between the small towns of Bacup and Todmorden, straddling the border between Yorkshire and Lancashire. Amazingly, one eighth of all alien contacts and abductions in the UK occurred within ten miles of this remote spot.

What further differentiated this window from Bonnybridge was that sightings of strange lights in the heavens stretch back to the days when horses and carts rather than cars and trucks, plied the Pennine roads. Strange encounters took place there even before the idea of flying saucers was invented. Local names link certain areas with supernatural encounters. Balls of light have been seen since medieval times over the Devil's Elbow, a desolate track in nearby Derbyshire. Near the town of Bacup is Pendle Hill, which was once believed to be home to 'demons', and those accused of being witches were put to the test by rolling them down its slopes. At the beginning of the twentieth century, a local constable reported seeing a strange 'airship' floating over Pendle Hill. Then in 1977, a car was stopped dead in its tracks by a UFO hovering in the mist on it summit.

All this has led UFOlogists to conclude that the Pennine window area is undoubtedly something real, while the one at Bonnybridge is actually a creation of media interest and speculation. UFOlogists point out that a similar 'window' opened in the London overspill development of Milton Keynes in Buckinghamshire in the 1970s. The sighting reports soared from practically nothing to dozens a year. However, when the statistics were analysed, it was discovered that this was because the population of the new town was soaring and there were simply more people around to report sightings.

The Pennine Triangle

On the 24 February 1979, Mike Sacks and his wife observed a strange orange object through the downstairs window of their home in the town of Bacup, one corner of the Pennine triangle. It lit up the room as it fell slowly and silently from the sky over Rossendale Valley. They observed the object as it descended, then it stopped, hovered for a bit, then changed course and shot off.

Sacks thought the object had landed in a nearby quarry and went out with his camera to investigate. When he got there, he heard a strange voice in his head that kept saying 'Portakabin, Portakabin'. As he looked down into the quarry he could see a set of lights which resembled those of a Portakabin. The next day when he returned to the site there was no Portakabin nor any other building that would have accounted for the lights.

Other people in the area, including two policemen, also reported seeing the strange object at around the time in question. Another witness, Alf Kyme, saw a dome-shaped mass surrounded by red rings descend into the quarry. A local taxi driver chased the object for a short while before losing it in the vicinity of the quarry.

The Ministry of Defence claimed that the sightings had been that of a 'special exercise' that had been taking place that night. However, Colonel Shrihofer, base commander at Upper Heyford, after checking his records said that there had 'definitely not' been any Air Force activity that night.

The last witness to see the UFO claimed that he saw the object while on Blackpool pier, and that he noticed an RAF jet chasing the object. The object then appeared to enter the sea and disappear. When the jet had disappeared, the witness claims that he saw the object rise from the sea and shoot off vertically.

UFO researchers will have to wait until the year 2009 before they can obtain any documents on the case, as the UK government hold all such documents for thirty years.

Silent Running

On 30 October 1975, military personnel at the Wurtsmith Air Force Base, Michigan, reported seeing what appeared to be running lights of low-flying craft. The craft hovered up and down and performed erratic zigzag manoeuvres.

The base received several calls from outside personnel who had also seen this strange object. All of them reported that they had seen the same craft and they said that it was completely silent in operation.

A pilot in a KC-135 tanker reported seeing the object as he was preparing to land. The pilot was ordered to change course and try to observe what the object was. Several times as the KC-135 approached to within a mile or so of the object it would suddenly shoot away at a tremendous speed; this happened three or four times before the pilot had to return because of a shortage of fuel. The pilot later estimated that the object had flown at over a thousand knots.

A Freedom of Information Act request managed to turn up the following entry in the NORAD log: 'Alerted by NCOC of a helicopter sighted over Wurtsmith AFB Wpns storage area, a tanker sighted same and pursued it 35° SE over Lake Huron. Upon request of NCOC – Gen Wainwright and concurrence of Gen Taylor – contacted 379BW CP and offered assistance. Also advised ML, LH and JL alert of possibility of a scramble.'

There were also several reports from civilians in nearby towns who had also witnessed the object that same night.

Down Under, Again

In the early morning of 30 September 1980, near Rosedale, Victoria, an Australian cattle rancher was awoken by the sound of his frightened cattle. When he went outside, he saw a domed disc with orange and blue lights gliding about ten feet above the ground. It rose slightly in the air, hovered briefly above an open ten-thousand-gallon water tank, and then landed fifty feet away.

The rancher jumped on his motorbike and sped towards the object, which was making a 'whistling' sound. Suddenly an 'awful scream' sounded as a black tube extended from the UFO's base. With an ear-splitting bang, the strange craft rose into the air. A blast of air knocked the rancher down.

The sounds ceased as the object slowly moved to a position about thirty feet away and eight feet above the ground. Hovering briefly, it dropped debris – stones, weeds, cow dung – from underneath it, then flew away, disappearing in the east.

A ring of black flattened grass thirty feet in diameter marked the place where the disc had landed. When he examined it in the daylight, the witness discovered that all the yellow flowers within the circle had been removed. Only green grass remained. But even more bizarre, the water tank was empty, with no evidence of spillage. Only the muddy residue at the bottom of the tank was left – and it had been pulled into a two-foot-high cone shape. The witness was sick with headaches and nausea for more than a week afterward.

A similar ring of blackened grass was found the following December at Bundalaguah, not far from Rosedale. The water in a nearby reservoir was also mysteriously missing.

Red Light

On 13 August 1960, near midnight, while driving east of Corning, California, state police officers Stanley Carson and Charles Scott saw a lighted object drop out of the sky. Fearing the imminent crash, they slammed on the brakes and jumped out of their car.

The object continued to fall until it reached about one hundred feet, at which point it suddenly reversed direction and climbed four hundred feet, where it stopped and began to hover. Carson wrote in his official report:

'At this time, it was clearly visible to both of us. It was surrounded by a glow, making the round or oblong object visible,' he said. 'At each end, or each side of the object, there were definite red lights. At times about five white lights were visible between the red lights. As we watched, the object moved again and performed aerial feats that were actually unbelievable.'

The two officers radioed the Tehama County Sheriff's Office and asked it to contact the nearest Air Force Base, which was at Red Bluff. Radar confirmed the object's presence.

The UFO remained in view for more than two hours. During that time, two deputy sheriffs and the county jailer made independent sightings.

'On two occasions the object came directly towards the patrol vehicle,' said Carson. 'Each time it approached, the object turned, swept the area with a huge red light. Officer Scott turned the red light on the patrol vehicle towards the object, and it immediately went away from us. We observed the object use the red beam approximately six or seven times, sweeping the sky and ground areas. The object began moving slowly in an easterly direction and we followed. We proceeded to the Vina Plains Fire Station where it was approached by a similar object from the south. It moved near the first object and both stopped, remaining in that position for some time, occasionally emitting the red beam. Finally, both objects disappeared below the eastern horizon.'

Carson also noted that each time the object came near they experienced radio interference. No one has ever explained this sighting.

Encounters in Michigan

On 20 March 1966, near Dexter, Michigan, farmer Frank Mannor and his son watched a car-sized, football-shaped object with a central porthole and pulsating lights at each end of its brown, quilted surface rise from a swampy area on his farm, hover for several minutes at a thousand feet, and then then depart.

The following day, eighty-seven women students at Hillsdale College in Hillsdale, Michigan, their dean and a civil defence director all claimed to have watched, for four hours, a glowing football-shaped object hovering above a swampy area several hundred yards from the women's dormitory. At one point, the object flew directly towards the dormitory, then retreated. On another occasion the object appeared to 'dodge an airport beacon light'. Its glow would diminish when police cars approached, and it 'brightened when the cars left'.

The Michigan sightings made nearly every newspaper. Even the *New York Times* – which normally declined to run 'flying saucer' stories – gave it several inches. Major Hector Quintanilla, head of the US Air Force's Project Blue Book, which investigated UFO sightings, sent Blue Book's scientific consultant astronomer Dr. J. Allen Hynek to Michigan to investigate.

'By the time I arrived,' Hynek later wrote, 'the situation was so charged with emotion that it was impossible to do any serious investigating. I had to fight my way through reporters to interview witnesses. Police were madly chasing stars they thought to be flying saucers. People believed space ships were all over the area.'

Hynek spent a week interviewing witnesses; he even pulled on a pair of hip boots to wade through farmer Frank Mannor's swamp. Pressure mounted for an explanation, and on 27 March Hynek held the largest press conference in the Detroit Press Club's history. Hynek later described the gathering of television reporters, newspapermen, photographers and others, all 'clamouring for a single, spectacular explanation of the sightings,' as 'a circus'.

Hynek provided 'what I thought at the time to be the only explanation possible… I made the statement it was "swamp gas".' This is a faint glow caused when decaying vegetation has spontaneously ignited. He went on to emphasise he could not prove this in a court of law and that there was another explanation, but the press had picked up the words 'swamp gas' even before he had finished and that was what was reported. Naturally Hynek's 'swamp gas' explanation met with ridicule and hostility, and increased suspicion that the government was engaged in a cover-up.

Victor Alert

On the 1 July 1977, the NATO base at Aviano, Italy, which was closed for flying because a parade was being prepared, had a close encounter. At about 3 a.m. a USAF guard observed a strange object hovering above an area known as 'Victor Alert', which housed two secret jet fighters in a large hanger. The object was described as a large spinning top, 150 feet in diameter and hovering very low above the hangar. The upper surface was domed and had white, red and green lights emitting from its surface.

The USAF guard reported the incident and a team of military guards were sent to the hangar. The guards surrounded the area and radar personnel were contacted to see if they could pick the object up on their equipment. However, when they tried to access the radar consoles, the base was hit by a mysterious power-cut.

The incident was reported all the way up to NATO headquarters in Brussels, but it was later dismissed as the moon shining off some low clouds.

Soviet Sightings

During the Cold War, little of what happened on the other side of Iron Curtain was known in the West. There was the lingering suspicion that UFOs were in some way linked to the titanic struggle between the Communist bloc and the Western democracies. Sightings were often dismissed as secret weapons developed either by the US or by the Soviets.

It was not until the summer of 1991, and the so-called 'Second Russian Revolution', when Mikhail Gorbachev was toppled and Boris Yeltsin began dismantling Soviet Union itself, that UFOlogists in the West got their first hint that the Russians had been plagued with similar encounters. Then, as the KGB opened up, files detailing UFO sightings that had taken place between 1982 and 1995 were released.

One of the most recent encounters had occurred on 3 February 1995. Private Schepin and Private Zhabanov of the Russian Army were on guard at a fuel-oil depot near the settlement of Guzev in the Burg region when they saw a luminous dot, flying parallel to the ground at no great height, for several minutes.

'Between 2200 and 2400 hours I was in charge of Post Two guarding the south-eastern side of the depot,' says Zhabanov in his official account. 'At about 2400 hours, while patrolling the prescribed route from the observation tower to the Post One border, I heard a faint click, similar to the sound of a cigarette case being closed. On hearing this faint click, I turned around to check if everything was OK, but as I saw nothing suspicious I decided to walk on.

'Having taken a few steps, I felt a bright light above me... What attracted my attention was a luminous dot of a greenish colour similar to a signal flare, with a tail like it was a comet. It moved at an altitude of about 18-20 metres from the ground parallel to the perimeter. I observed this – let's call it an object – for only a few seconds. Since the moment that I first saw it, it had flown some distance.'

Zhabanov was unable to make any realistic estimate of the distance the 'object' had travelled before it suddenly separated into two parts.

'One part seemed to go out when it separated from the main [body] and descended. The second, larger part, having flown a certain distance, also began to burn out, and, having turned into a small dot, then disappeared from sight.'

The following morning, two soldiers guarding another post at the depot saw something similar, although they said the object was blue. One of them, Warrant Officer Yarosh, described a ball of light flying above the depot. Interestingly, he also said that a similar series of events had occurred at the depot in December 1983. He had reported these incidents to his superior officers at the time, but they had been unable to come up with any explanation. They said that as far as they knew there were no experimental aircraft on manoeuvres in the area at the time.

Another incident was recorded in 1983. This time it was witnessed by a more high-ranking officer and Communist Party official. Colonel Skrypnik was the duty officer at a top-secret installation. Its exact whereabouts are still classified, as its name had been deleted from the document when it was released. However, it is clear that it was somewhere near the city of Kursk in central Russia.

Interviewed seven days after the event took place, 'Col. Skrypnik recounted that at 6 a.m. on 17 October [1983], Major Kiselev… reported a visual contact with a UFO that was sporadically moving, changing its altitude and brightness, and periodically emitting a beam of light directed downwards. The UFO was of a round shape with a bright halo around it and a darker centre. The UFO was moving randomly and had no definite direction. Observers sighted the appearance of periodic light beams directed towards the earth. On its closest approaches to the ground, the UFO looked like a polyhedron, invariably with a shining halo around it.

'A P-12 radar... did not manage to pick up the object and produce any valuable data. By means of a geodetic level sited at Kursk, the UFO was visually fixed, illuminated by the rays of the rising sun, at an elevation angle of about 30–50° above the horizon...

'All the UFO observers are positive that the object they watched was not identical to any star in the observation sector. This was proved by the UFO's random movement, with altitude and brightness variations, and the periodic light beam directed towards the earth. The UFO was sighted at sunrise, when no stars are visible.'

But it was not just Skrypnik, Kiselev and their comrades who had seen it. According to the report, the object was observed from several cities. The names and ranks of the people who made the sightings were given and the KGB worked out by triangulation that the UFO must have been hovering above the city of Voronezh, three hundred miles south-east of Moscow. Attached to the report are the statements of twelve eyewitnesses, apparently stationed there, that confirm this. Indeed, sightings of UFOs were a regular occurrence in Voronezh. In 1989, schoolchildren there said that a UFO had landed in one of the city's parks and contact was made, according to a report from the Russian news agency Tass on 9 October. The case was investigated by Vladimir Lebedev and Dr Henry Silanov. According to Silanov's report: 'In the period between September 21 to October 28 1989, in the Western Park, six landings and one sighting (hovering) were registered, with the appearance of walking beings. We have collected a wealth of video materials with eyewitness accounts, particularly from pupils of the nearest school. We have no doubt that they are telling the truth.'

Inspection of the landing site revealed 'incredibly high levels of magnetism'. Imprints found in the ground indicated that an object weighing around eleven tonnes had landed there.

On 23 May 1985, a UFO crashed into the forest at Khabarovsk in south-east Russia. The report says: 'The next day at 04:00 an anomalous phenomenon was observed for 10–12 minutes at the Litovoko bombing range... by the [censored] regiment senior navigator programmer Major V.V. Kudriavtsev and meteorological section engineer Senior Lieutenant V.V. Maltsev. The ellipsoid object with light beams leaving it upwards and downwards was of a dull white colour. The intensity of the lower beam was much greater than that of the upper one. The object was moving at a high altitude and a high speed.'

Another sighting came from the industrial town of Khabarovsk on the night of 5–6 May. Lieutenant Colonel Kornienko reported the encounter to the KGB:

'Between 01:20 and 01:26, I sighted a strangely "behaving" object in the north-eastern part of the sky at a fairly large distance from where I was standing. The object, the shape of a cigar or an ellipsoid, was flying fast in a vertical attitude. Sectors of light – I cannot call them beams – were leaving the bottom part of the object.'

A number of other Soviet UFO sightings took place near to military installations, where there were trained military observers. However, as during the Cold War any information about these bases would be highly sensitive, the files are distinguished by their poverty of detail. But nothing could be done to disguise a cigar-shaped object that was seen flying over the slopes of Mount Aj-Petri in the Crimea in September 1983. A flying 'silver ball' had been seen there five years before. These sightings remain officially unexplained. A large saucer-shaped UFO was photographed hovering over a church in Yaroslavl near Moscow in 1983. And in 1991, seventeen-year-old Alexandr Pavlov photographed a UFO flying over the Volga near the town of Tver in Central Russia. He was too far away to tell how big it was but said, as he watched, it changed in shape from a disc into a ball.

One of the most intriguing UFO sightings in the KGB files happened on 12 November 1985, when Hasan Kayumovich Rakhimov was on guard duty at a military installation inside the USSR known cryptically as 'Post Seven'. According to his account, 'a ball of yellow-blue colour, the size of a football, suddenly appeared... about 30–40 metres from where I stood'.

The UFO was initially spotted when it was thirty to fifty feet above the ground, but it seemed to bounce up and down as it hopped across the base. 'Having made three or four hops of 50–100 metres,' Rakhimov said, 'it moved towards the dog-breeding quarters and disappeared.'

This may sound like a ball lightning phenomenon, a common feature of Russian encounters. However, another UFO sighting that occurred a few weeks earlier in the same area punches a hole in this theory. On that occasion, two civilians were out hunting when they saw a UFO that could not be explained as ball lightning.

'At 20:30 on 3 November 1985, I returned to my motor boat and started the motor to warm it up,' one of the men reported. 'Then I caught sight of a UFO moving at high speed from the north to the south at an altitude greater than that of an aeroplane. The UFO was a little bit larger than a star, and had a searchlight beam leaving it at an angle of 5–10 degrees. The weather was clear, and the UFO was clearly visible against a starry sky.

'The light beam covered about a quarter to a fifth of the distance from the object to the ground. The beam did not hit the ground, but scattered. When the UFO came closer, the motor on the boat suddenly stopped. I thought that the jolting might have caused the lever to slip into reverse. I pulled the starter cord after I had checked the fuel and opened the throttle. The motor started at once, but as it was running I saw a glow coming out of the ignition coil sockets. Having run for five to seven seconds, the motor stopped again. And it stopped abruptly, without slowing down. The UFO at that time was overhead.

'After the UFO flew south in the direction of Vladivostok we saw a satellite above it. The UFO and the satellite moved with the same speed and in the same direction. Having flown for some time more, the searchlight was switched off and the UFO was no longer visible.'

According to the KGB documents, a large number of UFO sightings occurred over the far east of Russia. In 1986, a huge flying saucer was photographed over Iturup, the largest of the Russian Kuril Islands. The Kamchatka peninsula in the far eastern corner of the mainland of the Russian Federation was home to other sightings in 1987 and 1988. Personnel at the Kura Missile Range regularly reported 'the overflights of ball-shaped unidentified flying objects'. Private Kolosov and Senior Lieutenant Vasilevski at Telemetry Instrumentation Site Three saw a UFO that resembled 'climbing lights changing their colour from red to white'.

In a military report, Senior Lieutenant Vasilevski pointed out that sightings of the UFOs are correlated with the scheduled launch times of heavy missiles,' claiming that 'when the times were slipped, the objects would not appear'. Others did not make that connection. In mid-December 1987, two privates and a warrant officer saw an orange ball of light moving from the north to the south. Similar objects were seen on two other occasions that same month and at intervals over the following year. On the night of 9–10 September 1988, a silver ball emitting a cone-shaped beam of light down towards the earth was sighted five minutes before a missile launch. The UFO appeared to be the size of the moon when viewed from the earth.

Vasilevski's encounters were reported from three different locations and sightings lasted from thirty seconds to three minutes. The UFOs were also seen by officers stationed on the top of Lyzyk mountain, near the range's missile site. The testimony of these two officers is more important because they were trained observers. And as senior personnel, they had more to lose.

The sighting of UFOs over Russia and Soviet Central Asia continued in the final years of the Soviet Union. On 22 September 1989, in the south-west Russian city of Astrakhan, half-a-dozen individual witnesses saw a glowing, red 'drop-shaped' UFO near Koxhevaya railway station. Three other witnesses said the object was yellow, but had seen it on and off for forty-five to fifty minutes.

Six days later, near the runway of a nearby air base, two 'luminous, violet and red dots nearly a metre in diameter' were seen by several witnesses. A month later, another 'red drop' was seen by a large number of civilian and military witnesses near the village of Burkhala in the Yagodinski region.

Nine months before the Soviet Union collapsed, a handful of witnesses saw bright white flashes in the sky over the town of

Aleksandrov, not far from Moscow. They reported seeing them anything from four or five kilometres up to just a few metres off the ground. Their estimates of the speeds of these objects and descriptions of their flight patterns also varied widely. One was seen over the eternal flame in the Tomb of the Unknown Soldier in Karabavano. It seems that the UFO emitted a flash of light that momentarily lit up the monument.

Flying Triangles were also seen over the Soviet Union in March 1990. One was even photographed over the Russian town of Tagresk. Speculation was – as in the West – that it was some kind of experimental aircraft. But that would not explain why one attacked a radar station at Kuybishev, Samara, near the Tarta province in Russia on 13 September 1990. It was witnessed by Corporal S. Dudnik.

'I watched the approaching flight of a big, black triangular craft, each side about fifty feet in length,' he said. 'It landed after coming down vertically, rather slowly and making a rattling noise. The flash of light, which shattered the radar antennae behind me, came out of the middle of the object. I could see no opening there, but it seemed to be aiming at its target and I found myself directly in its line of fire. Oddly enough, nothing happened to me, but the antennae collapsed and began to burn brightly.' The team who inspected the collapsed radar antennae could not explain how the steel parts could have been melted by a beam of energy fired from 160 yards away.

On 3 March 1991, a diamond-shaped craft was photographed over the Tevare military base by a gang of local youths. It hovered menacingly before disappearing. Another strange diamond-shaped craft was caught on video by Nikolai Yegorov over the Crimean city of Sevastopol in August 1993. It shows the UFO accelerating from ground level to a high altitude, and disappearing within the space of a minute.

It is clear from these reports and others in the KGB files that the UFO sightings reported in the West throughout the years of the Cold War also occurred behind the Iron Curtain – and the Soviet authorities were just perplexed by them as their counterparts in the

West. The question remains for UFOlogists: Is this apparent lack of interest in UFOs by the authorities in the former Soviet Union and in the West simply because they do not believe in such things, or because they already know what they are and are not saying?

Certainly the KGB files contain little by the way of analysis and the Soviet authorities seem to have made little effort to follow up on the sightings. They do seem to take them seriously, though. The man charged to investigate them was the president of the State Security Committee, Commander Popovitch. A letter from Popovitch in the file outlines the official position.

'The State Security Committee [SSC] has never been engaged in systematic gathering and analysis of information on anomalous phenomena (the so-called Unidentified Flying Objects). At the same time the SSC of the USSR has been receiving statements from a number of persons and agencies on cases of observations of the above phenomena. We forward you copies of such statements. At an earlier date the same material was sent to the Central Machine Building Research Institute in the town of Kalingrad.'

The investigation went no further.

Encounter in Rendlesham Forest

East Anglia has been home to a great deal of UFO activity, especially during the Cold War, when a large number of Air Force personnel, both British and American, were stationed there. In 1980, an incident occurred in Rendlesham forest that became one of the most intriguing cases in the annals of UFOlogy. Rendlesham is a vast pine forest that lies to the east of the county town, Ipswich. It runs across Suffolk, hitting the coast at a spit called Orford Ness, which is just down the coast from the nuclear power station at Sizewell. The Ness is known for its lighthouse, but it is also home to other mysterious buildings. Although officially they were home to research on over-the-horizon radar, at the time it was thought that the US's largest and most secretive intelligence, the National Security Agency – America's equivalent of Britain's GCHQ – was conducting top secret experiments known as 'Cobra Mist' there, involving prototype 'Star Wars' weapons. Also in the area were the twin NATO air bases of Bentwaters and Woodbridge, which were rented from the RAF by the US Air Force and, during the Cold War, were manned exclusively by USAF personnel.

On the night of Christmas Day 1980, a UFO was spotted over Rendlesham forest by Gordon Levett, who lived in a remote cottage near the village of Sudbourne. He was out in the garden with his dog. When the dog began barking, Levett looked up to see the UFO flying towards him. He said it was shaped like an upturned mushroom, glowing with a greenish-white phosphorescent light. It stopped briefly and hovered directly above him, at about rooftop height. Then it glided silently on in the direction of RAF Woodbridge.

Shortly after Levett's sighting, in the early hours of 26 December, the Webb family were returning home from a Christmas party. They were driving down the B road that snakes gently through the woodland between the villages of Woodbridge and Orford. Suddenly they spotted a huge white light over the trees. Aircraft activity was common in the area. Both American Chinook helicopters and A-10 Thunderbolts regularly disturbed the peace, but this strange light appeared to be very different from normal air traffic. For one thing it was silent. The Webbs were puzzling what it might when it suddenly plunged into the woods.

US Air Force security patrolmen Budd Parker and John Burroughs were at the east gate of RAF Woodbridge that night. They saw the light in the sky which, they said, looked like a Christmas tree. When it crashed into the forest, they assumed that an aircraft had been downed. Then they realised something odd was going on. The object had not simply plunged earthwards. It drifted downwards, as if under control. There was no explosion as it hit the ground. Now was there any sense of impact. All they could see in the forest was a mass of flashing coloured lights.

Burroughs phoned base HQ. It was 2 a.m. and he was told that no aircraft should have been in the area at that time. Nevertheless, base security despatched Sergeant Jim Penniston to investigate in a jeep driven by Herman Kavanasac.

As the UFO had flown over, David Roberts and his girlfriend

had been enjoying a few moments of tenderness out on the grass under the trees. They had been hoping that the midwinter darkness would protect them from the prying eyes of any late-night passers-by. But suddenly the cloak of darkness was snatched from them as the sky filled with light. Then the earth moved for them as something heavy crashed into the ground less than half-a-mile away. They had barely had time to compose themselves when a military jeep came hurtling down the forest trail towards the crash site. Its lights were flashing and its sirens blaring. Something serious was going on. The romance of moment was lost and they fled.

Outside the east gate, Penniston and Kavanasac saw strange-coloured lights flickering through the trees. Penniston assumed command. He told Parker and Burroughs that this was an emergency. A plane had gone down in the forest and was burning furiously. But they were not convinced. As far as they were concerned, whatever was in the wood had landed, not crashed.

Penniston led Burroughs and Kavanasac out into the forest to investigate, leaving Parker manning the gate. As they made their way deeper into the wood, they found that radio contact with the base began to break down. Their communication was swamped with static as if they were in the presence of a massive electric field. So Penniston told Kavanasac to station himself at the edge of an access route, where the radio still worked. From there, he could act as a communications relay.

Penniston and Burroughs continued on into the woods. Penniston was convinced that they would find an aircraft ablaze in the forest but, as they approached a clearing, the air crackled with static electricity. The two men's skin began to tingle and their hair stood on end. In the clearing they saw, not tangled wreckage, but a strange craft. It was conical and, Penniston said, it hovered about a foot above the ground on beams of light, though other witnesses said it had legs. There were strange black markings on the side in some alien script and the whole object was bathed in a glowing aura.

'The air was filled with electricity,' said Penniston, 'and we saw an object about the size of a tank. It was made of moulded black glass and had symbols on it… It was definitely not in the Jane's Book of World Aircraft.'

Although he could not readily identify it, it was Penniston's job to find out what it was. So after a few moments gathering his thoughts, Penniston tried to approach the craft. But he and Burroughs found themselves in the grip of a force field. They said it was like trying to wade through molasses. They went through the motions of walking but could not seem to get any closer to the object.

Then suddenly there was a flash of light and the craft shot skywards. With this, the sleepy forest became alive with birds fleeing their roosts and deer bolting for cover. All the airmen could do was stand open-mouthed as they stared into the sky.

The morning after Penniston and Burroughs' close encounter in Rendlesham Forest, tangible evidence of the presence of a UFO was found. The tops of the trees had been smashed off, leaving a huge swathe through the forest as if something heavy had crashed from the sky. Gordon Levett's dog was found shivering in its kennel, terrified to come out. It became ill and the vet was called. He could only speculate that the dog had been poisoned. There was nothing he could do and, within a couple of days, the dog was dead.

An A-10 fighter flew over the site at dawn and detected a high level of radiation in the area. In the frozen soil at the landing site, three indentations were found. These matched the location of the beams or legs seen under the mysterious craft the night before. The area was surveyed in detail and plaster casts taken. However, the police showed little interest, dismissing the indentations as rabbits' holes. The Ministry of Defence made no effort to investigate. According to MoD UFO investigator Nick Pope, this was ruled out by the US authorities.

However, this was not the end of the matter. The following evening, there was a party for officers at RAF Bentwaters. Base commander Ted Conrad was about to make an after-dinner speech when acting night security commander Lieutenant Bruce Englund burst in to report that a security patrol near the Woodbridge road had seen strange lights floating in the sky over the forest. 'It' was back. Conrad ordered his deputy, Lieutenant Colonel Charles Halt, to make a thorough investigation. Halt quickly assembled a team of skilled airforce personnel and equipment. Halt grabbed a portable Dictaphone to take notes. Englund commandeered some gas-powered arc lights to illuminate the forest, and Sergeant Nevells of the 'Disaster Preparedness' unit carried a Geiger counter to measure radiation. John Burroughs also turned up to join the group.

Halt established a security cordon around the perimeter of the wood. The strange lights the security patrol had seen were no longer visible. Although he could not see the UFO, Halt had no doubts that it was still there. Just as Penniston and Burroughs had reported previously, radio communications – both between members of the team and with the base – were swamped with static and the security cordon had to serve as a relay. Halt also had trouble with the 'light-all' arc lights he had brought. They kept cutting out and he sent back to base for new ones.

In the gloom, there was nothing visible except for a few stars and the beam of the Orford Ness lighthouse and the Shipwash lightship to the south. Halt and his men knew the area well enough not to confuse these lights with UFO activity. Without any further sighting to go on, Halt began an accurate record of the situation and began making notes on his Dictaphone.

'One-hundred-and-fifty feet or more from the initial – I should say suspected – impact point. Having a little difficulty. Can't get the light-alls to work... Meanwhile we're gonna take some readings with the Geiger counter and, ah, chase around the area a little bit, waiting for another light-all to come out.'

In the background on the tape, the clicks of the Geiger counter could be heard soaring. The radiation levels rose to ten times the normal background level. This was significant, but just short of danger level, so Halt continued with his investigation.

The team began taking samples of tree bark and soil, and photographed the damage they found in the area. An infra-red night vision detector picked up heat or some form of energy. This activity went on for more than an hour.

Then, at 1:48 a.m., a group of men who had ventured deeper into the forest, including Burroughs and Sergeant Adrian Bustinza, spotted something. Bustinza described it as a glowing light resting on a pillar of yellowish mist and split in the middle like a rainbow produced by a prism. On the tape, Halt can be heard telling his men to 'slow down' and be careful. He, too, had seen the light.

'There's no doubt about it,' he said on the tape. 'There's some type of strange flashing red light ahead… It appears to be moving a bit this way. It's brighter than it has been. It's definitely coming this way. There's no doubt about it. This is weird.'

The light grew and changed shape. It began to look like a large eye with a dark pupil at its centre. Initially, Halt said he thought it must be a mirage or atmospheric phenomenon such as a temperature inversion. But as it moved through the forests he became convinced that this was no earthly phenomenon.

Halt and his group of airmen chased the light through the woods, across a farmer's field and over a small brook. For more than an hour they followed it, with Halt recording details of the encounter on tape: 'Zero three fifteen – now we've got an object about ten degrees directly south.'

Suddenly, without warning, the object soared into the air. After a moment of silence, Halt's quavering voice can be heard saying: 'Now we observe what appears to be a beam coming down towards the ground – this is unreal.'

By this time Halt's team were tired and wet. Some of them had forded a stream. So, with the strange lights still visible above RAF Woodbridge, they turned for home. As they reached the perimeter fence, they saw laser-like beams shining down into the security area. One beam hit the ground so close to Halt that he thought they were under attack. And it was not just the military personnel on the base who saw the beams. Local residents witnessed them too. Sarah Richardson, whose bedroom overlooked the air base, said she saw 'bands of rippling colour' in the night sky.

The military tried to hush the story up. But rumours began to circulate among radar officers at RAF Watton after USAF intelligence staff commandeered their radar record for the 1980 Christmas period. The reason given was that a UFO had crashed into forest.

Senior USAF officers had witnessed the event and they had even seen extraterrestrials floating in beams under the alien craft. Three days later, USAF intelligence officers collected the records from RAF Neatishead. On the night of 26 December, the radar there had also detected an unidentified flying object. It had created a furore in the control room when it returned no identification and seemed to outperform NATO's best planes. When it disappeared off the screen at phenomenal speed it prompted a major investigation.

The story of the Rendlesham forest encounter leaked to the world of UFOlogy when, in January 1981, local paranormal researcher Brenda Butler was contacted by an American friend who was a USAF security police officer at Bentwaters and Woodbridge. He claimed that in the early hours of 26 December, he and two other guards had been sent into Rendlesham forest. There had been reports of a flying light crashing into the woods. When the men arrived they found a disc-shaped craft on tripod legs resting on the ground. They radioed back to the base for back-up and over the next couple of hours senior personnel came out to the site. But Butler's friend also reported that several small aliens, about three feet tall with grey skin and large heads, were seen floating around the craft as if making repairs. He also claimed that one of the senior officers tried to communicate with the aliens using sign language.

Together with UFO researchers Jenny Randles and Dot Street, Butler started collating eyewitness evidence and testimony. The three of them put together a book on the incident called *Sky Crash*. Its publication opened the floodgates. New witnesses came forward. One of the witnesses was a forestry worker, who stumbled onto the crash site a day after the crash. He said he reported the damage to the trees and the indentations on the ground to the local authorities. But when he returned the next day, the entire site had been cleared. The trees had been felled and the ground dug up.

The publication of *Sky Crash* alerted American UFO researchers, who eventually managed to obtain a secret memo on the incident through the Freedom of Information Act. The memo was written by Lieutenant Colonel Charles Halt. The circulation codes showed that it had been sent to Britain's Ministry of Defence as early as 13 January 1981 – although the MoD had told Jenny Randles that no such memo existed.

Halt's memo detailed three separate events. The landing of a small craft on the first night, the discovery of ground traces with excess radiation readings and another sighting the following night, which Halt himself had witnessed.

There is no doubt that Lieutenant Colonel Charles Halt was an extremely reliable witness. A professional soldier, he had been stationed in Japan and served in Vietnam. Soon after the Rendlesham incident, he was promoted to full colonel. Later, as commander of Bentwaters air base, he oversaw the deployment and, later, the decommissioning of cruise missiles there. He then took a staff job in the Pentagon before retiring in 1992 to take a job in the aviation industry.

The Halt memo also mentions a second document about the case. This has not been cleared for release to UFO researchers on the grounds of 'national security'.

Gordon Levett came forward with the tale of his sighting and the death of his dog. And a radar operator from the tracking station at RAF Watton told researchers that two days after the incident, USAF personnel came to the tracking station and removed all radar recordings for the previous two nights. These were never seen again.

All this new information, along with a transcript of the tape recording made by Halt on the night of the encounter, were put together by Jenny Randles in a second book, *From Out of the Blue*.

The other USAF airmen involved in the incident – Penniston, Burroughs, Bustinza and others – have since left the service and have spoken out. One of them was Larry Warren, a USAF security policeman who had been posted to England on 1 December 1980, just weeks before the incident.

'I was taken off my post to the forest,' he said, 'with a number of other personnel who were bringing lighting equipment out used to illuminate large areas, but it wouldn't work because of some mechanical malfunction. We still had no idea what we were up to.'

It was then that Warren saw a light moving through the forest.

'A dim red light, opposite the Orford lighthouse, stopped over a strange mist on the ground. It quickly transformed into a triangular object approximately thirty feet high. It had a solid structure, with a rough surface.'

Warren said that some men ran away. He, and others, stayed put. He said he could not move, but does not know whether that was because of shock or some external force.

'It was very dreamlike… I think time was distorted and perceptions were intentionally affected by this intelligence. There was one reality and in front of you was another. I felt slower on that night. Everything was on half speed and something was wrong; something was out of place.'

In all, some thirty military personnel, including senior officers, were all sent out into the forest to investigate. They all report witnessing something remarkable. Whatever they saw, they are convinced that it could not have been a plane crash or a secret aircraft downed in the woods, as it hit the forest then took off again. It was also seen to perform manoeuvres that seemed to defy the normal laws of physics. Some of the witnesses even claimed that they saw beams of light pass through jeeps and trees as if they were transparent.

So was the object in the forest a craft from another world? The witnesses do not rule out that possibility, but they say they cannot prove it. Was the craft under intelligent control? Some feel that some fantastic energy force, of unknown origin, might have created a natural UFO. A few think that a portal to a different dimension might have opened briefly under the influence of some natural earth energy.

Clifford Stone, a former US government intelligence agent, came up with a more intriguing theory. He claims that the Pentagon considers the Rendlesham forest incident presents some of the most persuasive evidence that we are not alone. He believes that the aliens that were seen 'did not originate on earth' and they were 'intruders from a parallel dimension – coming through a breach in the quantum basis of matter.'

On the other hand, sceptics, such as astronomer Ian Ridpath, says that all the witnesses saw was a bright meteor that crossed the skies of East Anglia around 2:50 a.m. This had lured the security personnel into the forest. Once there, the American airmen, who were unfamiliar with Suffolk surroundings, mistook the beam from the lighthouse on Orford Ness four miles away for a UFO. Ridpath maintains that the Rendlesham case is 'a ghastly embarrassment to UFOlogy'.

A bright meteor did indeed fly across south-east England on the night of 26 December. It was seen by numerous observers. But both the sighting report by Penniston and Burroughs and the testimony of the civilian witnesses show that they saw the UFO well before the meteor flew by at 2:50 a.m. Indeed, it has been suggested that the 'meteor' might even have been the UFO departing. Both Penniston and Burroughs say they saw the lighthouse as well as the UFO. They had been posted to the area for some time. Burroughs, particularly, liked to picnic in the woods and was familiar with the lighthouse.

Eyewitness Charles Halt also rejected Ridpath's theory. 'A lighthouse doesn't move through a forest,' he said. 'It doesn't explode, doesn't change shape, doesn't send down beams of light.'

Nevertheless, Ridpath was joined by other critics, including psychologist Nicholas Humphrey. In a Channel Four documentary and the pages of *New Scientist* magazine, he argued that what the witnesses saw was actually the flashing light on a police car that was called into the forest to investigate the crash. The problem was that the police car went to the forest in response to the airmen's sighting and, consequently, arrived after them.

Other sceptics say that the airmen saw a Russian rocket that re-entered the earth's atmosphere that night. Astronomer John Mason confirms that a 'brilliant natural fireball' caused by the rocket burning up was seen by many in south-east England. Others say that a Soviet satellite fell to earth over East Anglia that night and that it may even have been shot down by the Star Wars weapons being tested at secret establishments in the area.

The possibility has been raised that there was some nuclear

accident at one of the airbases and the military cooked up the UFO story to cover their tracks. At the time, the MoD denied that there were nuclear weapons at RAF Bentwaters, but more than ten years later admitted that there were.

However, this does nothing to explain what Penniston and Burroughs saw. They say they came very close to a craft that was like nothing they had ever seen before – and Halt and others saw the same thing the next night. Burroughs does not claim to have any answers, but insists: 'I do not know whether this was some kind of machine under intelligent control or a fantastic natural phenomenon – some rare kind of energy. What I do know is that it was nothing mundane. There are no words that can adequately describe the wonder of what we saw.'

Neither Burroughs nor Penniston were told the results of the investigation into the incident. Within hours, they were out of the loop. Halt discussed the case with his RAF liaison officer, Squadron Leader Donald Moreland. After that meeting, there was a publicity clampdown. Soon top-secret flights were landing at the air bases, bringing in personnel from America's covert intelligence agencies.

Retired Chief of Staff at the Ministry of Defence Admiral Lord Hill-Norton questioned the Defence Minister Lord Trefgarne about the incident and was told simply that there were no defence implications to the case. Similarly Michael Heseltine, Minister of Defence in the Thatcher government, said: 'There is not a grain of truth in the allegation that there has been a cover-up about alleged UFO sightings.'

However, Ralph Noyes, former under-secretary at the Ministry of Defence who headed the division that investigated UFO sightings, said that that was exactly what had happened.

'We now have the evidence – I blush to say about my own Ministry of Defence – that they have lied about this case,' he says. 'They have covered up.'

Sky Serpents

Even stranger things can be seen in the sky. In the early months of

1994, Santiago Ytturia had seen numerous UFOs in the skies over his hometown Monterrey in north-east Mexico and he was determined to capture one of them on film. So on 19 March 1994, Santiago Ytturia set up his video camera in the garden of his home and waited.

He kept his eyes on the skies but, after more than an hour of waiting, nothing happened. He was just about to give up, when his vigil was rewarded. Suddenly, a flashing light appeared in the sky. But as fast it had appeared, it disappeared again, leaving Ytturia bewildered. He waited for it to re-appear. He waited and waited, in vain. Eventually, Ytturia took down his camera. Then he went inside and replayed the video, just to see if he had captured the fleeting sighting. Sure enough, on reviewing the footage carefully, frame by frame, he saw the image of the glowing UFO. But as he checked the rest of the tape he found something even more intriguing.

A few frames after the fleeting appearance of the UFO, Ytturia noticed a brief but distinctive image. It was a long, spear-shape object, which flew across the screen at incredible speed. Analysing the footage a frame at a time, he calculated that the object was moving much too fast to be an insect or bird. Indeed, it could only be seen at all when the video was reviewed using stop frame. Ytturia was quickly convinced that he had captured something unique on film. What it was, he did not know. Nor did he know how it was linked to the recent UFO activity.

The phenomenon that Ytturia captured on video has since been dubbed a 'rod'. On careful analysis of other footage, similar anomalous objects have been discovered on videos filmed all around the world and a number of leading UFOlogists have turned their attention to the study of rods. One of the key figures in the investigation is Jose Escamilla. The owner of a video production company, Escamilla and his team of independent investigators have obtained spectacular footage and photographs of rods from countries around the world, including the UK, the US, Mexico, Canada, Sweden and Norway. Although they are usually seen flying through the air at incredible speeds, Escamilla also has film of rods underwater.

Despite the copious footage, the appearance of rods is so fleeting that little is known about them. However, what researchers have agreed upon so far is that rods are organic. These UFOs are living creatures and not just some new form of alien craft.

As sightings of rods have regularly coincided with UFO activity, some researchers believe that they are some sort of extra-terrestrial life form. Others believe that they may be an as-yet undiscovered type of terrestrial life. Naturally, sceptics have dismissed the sightings as stray insects, birds, lens flares or even camera trickery.

Detailed examination of the video footage has revealed several consistent features. The creatures are cigar-shaped and range in length from approximately four inches to about ten feet. Amazingly, they travel at speeds of up to 190 miles an hour, propelled by a solid, undulating membrane along each side of their body which vibrates extremely rapidly.

Jim Peterson, the Assistant State Director of MUFON in Colorado and another rods investigator, says: 'Rods are very hard to see with the naked eye. Usually, they are so fleeting and so fast that the brain just filters them out of your vision. Consequently, they have been virtually invisible until the recent advent of camcorders, where their presence has generally been captured accidentally.'

Even with thirty frames per second (fps), state-of-the-art video cameras still have difficulty in capturing detailed pictures of rods because of their enormous speeds. Within just a few frames they are gone. Even in the frames where they appear, their fantastic speeds mean that they appear as little more than a blur, so it is impossible to work out the details of their morphology. So far, it has not been possible to make out whether they have a head or eyes. Escamilla plans to obtain a special camera that can shoot 500 fps, rather than the 30 fps. At that speed, you can freeze the motion of a speeding bullet, so investigators should be able to determine more about the creatures' structure.

However, Escamilla has already been able to dismiss the cavils of critics. Rods can easily be distinguished from lens flares, he says, and lens flares do not manoeuvre around the frame when the camera is static. He has also shot rods footage that has insects, birds and rods all in the same frame. With a shutter speed of 1/10,000th of a second, he points out, the flight of an insect or bird is frozen, so you can easily make out what it is. But the flight of rods is so fast that the shutter can't freeze their motion and all you get is a blurred streak. However, it is just possible to see the undulating membranes that run down each side of rods' bodies. Escamilla says that these establish that, whatever these creatures are, they are not any known biological organism. His problem is to find out just what they are.

One extraordinary piece of video footage shows just how fast rods can fly. It was shot at a military gunnery range in Sundsvall, Sweden. A tank was filmed loosing off eight rounds in three seconds. As the tank fires, the shell casings are ejected through the top of the turret. A rod flashes through the frame and is gone before the first casing hits the ground.

The best video footage showing rods was shot by TV cameraman Mark Lichtle. In 1996, he was filming base jumpers parachuting into a deep ravine in Mexico. As in most cases involving rods, no one noticed them at the time. It was only when he ran the video back in slow motion that Lichtle saw swarms of rods darting in and out of the frame. They flew around the base jumpers as they free-falled into the ravine. In one shot, a rod is seen veering away at the last second to avoid colliding with one of the jumpers.

Lichtle's footage was examined by optical expert Dr Bruce Maccabee, who also analysed the Gulf Breeze UFO footage. He calculated that the objects were between six and twelve feet long – far too large to be either an insect or a bird.

In 1997, Escamilla presented his selection of footage to zoologists and entomologists from the University of Colorado. 'They were totally baffled by what they saw,' he says. 'All they could say was that it was unlike anything they had ever seen and that it deserved further study.'

Because there were so many rods in the ravine, Escamilla believes that it is some form of habitat for the creatures and, consequently, the ideal place to film and study them. Biologist Ken

Swartz took up the challenge and has been investigating the phenomenon since 1998.

'Rods appear to be biological,' he says, 'but without a physical specimen it is difficult to say anything conclusively. They seem to be amphibious, as they have been seen entering and leaving water. Perhaps they are born in the sea and emerge into the air?'

Swartz has discovered some eyewitness testimony of people who claim to have seen them on the ground. This seems to indicate that they have some similarities to the family of creatures known as cephalopods. 'There have been descriptions of them expanding like a balloon and rapidly deflating,' he says, 'so they could be using a mechanism similar to a squid, which sucks in water and jets it out for propulsion.'

What puzzles Swartz most is the creatures' enormous speed. This would mean that it would have to have a phenomenal metabolic rate. 'Even a hummingbird's incredibly rapid metabolic rate would still be nowhere near as fast as that of a rod,' he says. 'I estimate it would have to consume its own weight in food every day.'

Another problem is that, if they are biological entities, how come no one has found the body of a dead one? The video footage indicates that they are quite common, yet not a single dead body has been discovered on the ground. 'One feasible explanation,' says Swartz, 'is that, like a squid, they have no hard body parts and so could decompose without a trace.'

Undeterred by the lack of physical evidence, Swartz has turned to the evolutionary record for clues. 'If you look at the fossil record,' he says, 'there is only one creature that ever lived that had the rod mode of locomotion, and this was the dominant predator of the time called anamalocaris, which lived in the sea during the Cambrian evolutionary expansion four hundred million years ago.' According to Swartz, the creature propelled itself by a row of plates or fins that vibrated in a similar manner to the membranes seen on rods. From this, he concludes: 'It is possible that anamalocaris is the evolutionary ancestor of rods.'

Another evolutionary theory has been floated by British entomologist Dr Steven Wooten. He worked with palaeobiologists to create a theoretical reconstruction of original ancestors of modern-day insects. The creature they came up with was related to the now-extinct anamalocaris and is called a protopterygote. 'This creature looks amazingly like a rod,' says Jim Peterson. 'It is possible then that rods originally evolved from anamalocaris through this ancestor of insects and then took its own evolutionary path.' As yet, no one is sure.

Another remarkable piece of footage was shot on 3 May 1999, by meteorologist Garry England, when he was filming a tornado in Oklahoma for the local TV channel News Nine. When he reviewed the tape, he saw a rod flying towards the tornado at a height of around three thousand feet. It was about ten foot long and was seemingly unaffected by the 450-miles-per-hour wind. 'If these creatures are alive, they must be incredibly durable,' said England. 'The wind did not even slow it down.'

2 Near Misses and Encounters

Near Misses

The end of its routine two-hour flight from Milan on 6 January 1995 took British Airways flight BA 5061 though the UK's UFO hotspot over the south Pennines. It was already dark as it began its descent into Manchester Airport. The time was 6:48 p.m. and the Boeing 737 was flying at about four thousand feet as it prepared to turn towards runway 24. First officer Mark Stuart was monitoring the instruments, while Captain Roger Wills battled a strong north-westerly wind at the controls. Neither were prepared for what happened next.

The UFO flashed by at high speed, missing the right side of the aircraft by as little as three feet. In less than three seconds it was gone. The ashen-faced first officer turned to the Captain and said, 'Did you see that?' Captain Wills had indeed seen the object. Fortunately, due to the restricted view from the small side windows, none of the passengers had.

'I saw something out of my peripheral vision,' said Stuart. 'My instinct was to grab the controls as it seemed to be coming towards us. But I was unable to move more than an inch before it was upon us and past us.'

The crew called the tower at Manchester airport and asked if there were any other aircraft in the vicinity. Air traffic control reported that they could see no other plane on the radar screen. When the plane landed safely at Manchester, the crew sat down to discuss whether they should file an 'air miss' report. They were in broad agreement about what they had seen and decided to go ahead. Their report says: 'The first officer… looked up in time to see a dark object pass down the side of the aircraft at high speed; it was wedge-shaped with a black stripe.'

The pilots also attached sketches of what they saw, drawn minutes after they landed. First Officer Stuart drew a silver wedge-shaped craft with streaks along the side. Captain Wills saw it more as a series of lights, but agreed that the UFO was wedge shaped. Now it was up to the Civil Aviation Authority to find out what had nearly knocked them out of the sky.

The story was leaked to the press and made front-page news, especially as the UFO had also been seen from the ground by Manchester student Mark Lloyd, who said it was 'the size of Wembley stadium'. Wills and Stuart declined to give interviews, while the CAA struggled to come up with some plausible explanation. But with no reasonable answers to hand, eventually, even the CAA began speculating about UFOs – this is thought to be the first time an official air miss report mentioned 'extraterrestrial activity'. However, the CAA refused to go too far down that alley, saying: 'Fascinating though it may be, it is not within the [air miss] group's remit and must be left to those whose interest lies in that field.' But the fact that the CAA even mentioned the possibility of UFOs caused a storm in the tabloids. It was taken to mean that the plane had actually encountered aliens.

There could, of course, have been other explanations. The crew of BA 5061 might have encountered a bright fireball meteor, known as a bolide. Or it could have seen a piece of space debris falling back into the earth's atmosphere and burning up. These often cause strange lights high in the atmosphere.

But it may be that BA 5061 had a narrow escape that night. On 24 August 1984, a Britten-Norman Trislander operated by Kondair was on a cargo flight from London Stansted to Amsterdam when it was struck by an unidentified flying object with such force that it lost an engine. The aircraft managed to fly on to Schiphol, where it was forced to make an emergency landing. Once safely on the ground, the plane was examined. There was a large hole in the tail fin where something had passed right through. It was not a bird strike, as anomalous metallic fragments were discovered there.

The civil aviation authorities in the UK and Holland could come up with no explanation. The Ministry of Defence was brought in, in case some sort of military technology might have been involved, but they were equally baffled. Again there was speculation that the plane had been hit by space debris re-entering the atmosphere, but that would have been a billion-to-one freak event. But something had hit the aircraft. Although it had survived, next time a plane might not be so lucky.

There has been a long history of aerial sightings that cannot be easily explained. Until World War II, the skies were virtually empty. But with the war there were suddenly thousands of aircraft in flight over Europe and the Pacific on bombing raids and reconnaissance missions every night. Soon there were numerous reports of strange lights that appeared to tail Allied aircraft. These mysterious lights – usually only a foot or so in diameter – littered the skies as if they were observing the great aerial battles, yet they never interfered. The US Army Air Force, as it was then, dubbed them 'foo fighters', after the euphemistic expletive use by the character Smokey Stover in a popular American newspaper comic strip. It was only after the war that they discovered German and Japanese pilots were seeing foo fighters too.

Even after the end of the war, American military aircraft continued to report encounters with foo fighters, though they soon became known as UFOs. On 24 July 1948, two experienced Eastern Airlines crew members, pilot Clarence S. Chiles and his co-pilot, John B. Whitted, while en route from Houston to Atlanta, encountered a one hundred-foot-long, wingless, finless, cigar-shaped object with two rows of large, square windows that emanated a bright, glowing light from within.

On a seeming collision course with the UFO, Chiles threw his DC-3 airliner into a tight left-hand banking turn, and the object, with a forty-foot orange red flame flashing from its tail, shot past not more that seven hundred feet away. The object was tracked on radar and no explanation of the sighting has ever been given.

In 1952, there was a spate of anomalous sightings. On 14 July, two long-serving Pan American pilots encountered UFOs as they flew over Washington, D.C. They reported that the craft behaved in a controlled manner. Then, between 19 July and 26 July, the D.C. area was invaded by numerous UFOs, which were picked up on radar screens. Because of the possibility of a security threat to the Pentagon and the White House, a full investigation was ordered.

When the news reached British Prime Minister Winston Churchill on 28 July, he wrote to the Secretary of State for Air, Lord Cherwell, asking, 'What does all this stuff about flying saucers amount to? What is the truth?' He was about to find out.

Military Encounters

Between 19 September and 21 September 1952, the NATO manoeuvre Operation Mainbrace over England was intercepted by UFOs and, in the North Sea, an aircraft carrier carrying nuclear weapons was buzzed by a strange disc.

One of the most compelling cases occurred on the first day of the exercise, 19 September 1952, when two RAF officers and three aircrew at RAF Topcliffe observed a strange object which appeared to be following a Meteor jet. In a written statement, Flight Lieutenant John Kilburm wrote:

'The Meteor jet was crossing from east to west when I noticed the white object in the sky. This object was silver and circular in shape, about ten thousand feet up some five miles astern of the aircraft. It appeared to be travelling at a lower speed than the Meteor but was on the same course.

'I said "What the hell's that?" and the chaps looked to where I was pointing. Somebody shouted that it might be the engine cowling of the Meteor falling out of the sky. Then we thought it might be a parachute. But as we watched the disc maintained a slow forward speed for a few seconds before starting to descend. While descending it was swinging in a pendulum fashion from left to right.

'As the Meteor jet turned to start its landing run the object appeared hung in the air, rotating as if on its own axis. Then it accelerated at an incredible speed to the west, turned south-east and then disappeared. It is difficult to estimate the object's speed. The incident happened within a matter of fifteen to twenty seconds. During the few seconds that it rotated we could see it flashing in the sunshine. It appeared to be about the size of a Vampire jet aircraft at a similar height.

'We are all convinced that it was some solid object. We realised very quickly that it could not be a broken cowling or parachute. There was not the slightest possibility that the object we saw was a smoke ring or was caused by the vapour trail from the Meteor or from any jet aircraft. We have, of course, seen this, and we are all quite certain that what we saw was not caused by vapour or smoke. We are also quite certain that it was not a weather observation balloon. The speed at which it moved away discounts this altogether. It was not a small object which appeared bigger in the condition of light. Our combined opinion is that it was something we had never seen before in a long experience of air observation.'

This, along with other reports during 1952, caused the RAF to recognise UFOs officially.

On 3 March 1953, USAF Captain Roderick Thomspon was flying a F-84 strike aircraft during combat manoeuvres over Luke Air Force Base in Arizona. He and two student fliers saw a crescent-shaped UFO leaving a vapour trail. He attempted pursuit but could not catch it, but he did manage to capture it on his gun camera. The footage was only released in 1978 under the Freedom of Information Act.

On 23 November 1953, a USAF F-89 Scorpion was scrambled from Kinross Air Force Base to intercept a UFO. At 11:35 p.m. the plane intercepted the intruder. The two radar blips merged into one and the airbase lost radio contact with the plane. Then the radar blip disappeared too. Eventually the air controller had to file an accident report. An extensive land and water search found no trace of the craft or the two men aboard, pilot Lieutenant Felix Moncla, Jr, and radar observer Lieutenant R.R. Wilson.

Later, after aviation writer Donald E. Keyhoe broke the story in his 1955 best-seller *The Flying Saucer Conspiracy*, the Air Force insisted that the UFO had proved to be a Royal Canadian C-47. They claimed that the F-89C had not actually collided with the Canadian transport plane, but that something 'unspecified' had happened, and the interceptor crashed.

In 1958, a leaked Air Force document made it clear that officials considered the Kinross incident a UFO encounter of the strangest kind. The document quoted the radar operator as saying: 'It seems incredible, but the blip apparently just swallowed our F-89.'

In August 1956, over the UK, there were two UFO encounters within a week. A USAF transport plane flying at five thousand feet over East Anglia saw a smudgy yellow light below them. Radar systems in the area also detected a strange object moving between the air bases at RAF Bentwaters and RAF Lakenheath. Two RAF Venom fighters were scrambled and intercepted the UFO above Ely where, the pilots say, it hung stationary in the sky. Even so, try as they might, their weapons systems could not lock on to it.

A few days later, Flight Officer Wilbur Wright was one of two Javelin pilots who were flying a practice mission over the sea between the Isle of Wight and Bournemouth. They were ordered to break off their manoeuvre and to intercept a target picked up by a secret radar site nearby. This time the pilots managed to lock on to the UFO. When they came within visual contact range, they saw a bright disc which reflected the sun. It appeared to be hovering there, waiting for them to fly right at it. As the two planes closed within a few miles, the UFO simply flipped on its edge and took off into the sky at an incredible speed. In the blink of an eye, it had completely disappeared.

A UfO photographed over Mount Aso, Japan, on 21 December 1961 at 16:35. One of the needle-shaped clouds launched a dark sphere that came up to airliner JAL flight 307 from Tokyo to Fukuoka. Photographed by a member of the DC-4 crew.

A USAF F-106 intercepted a UFO over Masawa, Japan, in 1959. When the alien craft did not respond to his hails, the pilot was authorised to fire a warning shot. The pilot loosed a missile, then began screaming that it had no effect. He said that the UFO was now pursuing him and it was closing rapidly. His last radio message said that the UFO had turned some kind of beam on him. The radio fell silent. On the radar screen, the blips from the F-106 and his pursuer merged – and disappeared.

Many similar cases defy any rational explanation. In September 1976, a UFO was seen by many people over the outskirts of Tehran. An Iranian Air Force Phantom was scrambled to intercept it. As the pilot approach what he took to be a glowing light, he noticed a small object eject from it. Thinking that he might be under attack, he prepared to launch an air-to-air missile. But just as he pressed the button to fire, all power drained from his aircraft. The object he had seen returned into the UFO, then the Phantom's electrical system powered up again. An explanation is that the UFO was an intelligent craft with capabilities that far outstrip our own.

'They've tested our defences to see if we can withstand an invasion... at some time in the future we can expect UFOs to become increasingly hostile,' a CIA informant told a journalist.

Soviet Encounters

On 20 October 1982, a Soviet Illyushin-62 Airliner, flying from Moscow to Magadan on the Siberian coast, was forced to make an unscheduled stop at Petropavolovsk in Kazakhstan, as the weather had closed in at its destination. The plane was on its final approach, when the crew saw 'a shining object flying at head-on and parallel headings, and various speeds and flight levels.' The pilot, Captain Vasilievyh, and others on the flight deck watched the object for over twelve minutes. However, neither their radar nor that of air traffic control on the ground were able to detect the object. Vasilievyh said: 'We are observing flashes but there is nothing on the radar, but the light flashes with a ten-second period.' And he clearly identified the object as 'some alien flying object'.

Vasilievyh told Karikov, the air traffic controller at

Petropavolovsk: 'At a flight level of about 7,200 metres I caught sight of two intermingling, bright blue lights, 45 degrees to port and below us. I thought that it was an incoming plane and flashed the lamps for it and then reported to the air controller that there was an incoming plane below me. The controller told me that the zone was clear and that no planes were present. After that I saw the shining object several times, but now it was of a light yellow colour which seemed to burn for about 25–30 seconds... first the object was moving towards me from the port, then it stopped and started moving away at 80 degrees off our heading.'

According to the files, eight minutes after the aircraft landed, Karikov 'saw due north, exactly along the projection of the runway, a burst of light resembling the flasher of an aircraft. He observed six bursts during three minutes; the colour of the bursts varied from pink-red to pink, first in the western and then in the north-western direction.' When the aircraft was given a routine inspection five days later, serious damage to the engine was found.

Another encounter involved an airliner flying from Volgograd to Tbilisi in Georgia on 14 December 1987. The crew reported a 'flying object on a head-on course, resembling an aircraft with retracted landing lamps burning'. Another airline crew said: 'The UFO was also observed by tail number 6352 which reported the sighting at about 23:20. The crew reported a fire train scattering sparks that was trailing the UFO.'

An unnamed witness phoned the air traffic controller at the local airport and reported seeing an object like a 'burning aeroplane trailing a tail of fire flying over the settlement. After a light-burst resembling an explosion – although there were no accompanying sound effects – the aircraft disappeared.' But the caller could see 'no debris or explosion after-effects'. There were no reports of any crash debris being found.

The KGB files carry the following conversion between the air traffic controller at Sochi Airport on the Black Sea and the aircrew of Flight 138 after the airliner had been buzzed by UFOs:

Air Traffic Controller: TWR Flight 138. Go ahead.

Flight 138: Request you observe two objects hanging on our port.
Air Traffic Controller: What altitude to your port?
Flight 138: Our altitude, 50 or 60 kilometres directly abeam.
Air Traffic Controller: You have head-on traffic. Do you observe anything to port?
Flight 138: There was one object, then another one appeared nearby. Now they are flying away from us. The distance is already about 80 kilometres.
Air Traffic Controller: What is their shape?
Flight 138: One is oblong, the shape of a dirigible. The other is kind of spherical.

Russian planes even got buzzed on the ground. In 1990, three UFOs flew low over an Illyushin-96-300 standing at an airfield near Moscow, leaving vapour trails. A witness, Nikolay Nilov, managed to photograph the mysterious objects, but the entire incident remains unexplained.

Aerial encounters were also reported by Soviet military aircraft. One KGB file says: 'On 23 May 1985, during the scheduled flights of the 27th Bomber Regiment over Khabarovsk, an unidentified flying object the shape of an ellipsoid was observed at 22:35 local time in the vicinity of the airfield. The pale orange UFO was moving from the west to the east at a speed of 500–600 kilometres an hour and at an altitude of 2–3 kilometres. A glow in the form of a halo was visible around the object.'

The report goes on to state that 'the object's movement was not accompanied by noise of any kind. No target bursts were observed on radar scopes. No adverse effects on personnel, hardware or environment were registered.' Although statements such as this are common throughout the KGB files, some UFOlogists have speculated that they imply that, on other occasions, 'adverse effects' on personnel, hardware or the environment were registered, but that these incidents have been suppressed.

These encounters are not without their dangers. In 1961, an Antonov AN-2P mail plane disappeared from the radar between

Ekaterinburg in the Sverdlovsk region and Kurgan in western Siberia. A UFO was being tracked in the area at the time. A Red Army helicopter found the plane in a small clearing in dense forest. The plane was intact and it had not cut a swathe through the trees as it had come into land. It appeared to have been dropped there from above. There was no sign of the seven people who were on the plane. However, there was a scorched circle of grass a hundred feet in diameter, around a hundred yards from the plane.

Mexican Wave

During the wave of sightings over Mexico City in the 1990s, the Mexican government refused to make any official comment on the UFO question. This may be because UFOs buzzing Mexico City presented a clear danger to aeroplanes using the city's international airport and they did not want to cause panic among passengers. The danger was highlighted on the evening of 28 July 1994, when Flight 129 was making its final approach into Mexico City airport. The DC9 had 109 passengers on board. They had just settled back for a routine landing when the plane was hit by a unknown object.

'I've never felt an impact so strong,' said the captain, Raymond Cervantes Ruana. 'When we checked the plane we discovered that one of the shock absorbers had been ripped off.'

Following the mid-air collision, Ruana had to make an emergency landing, but he managed to get the aircraft down safely. Once the passengers had been evacuated, Ruana rushed to the control tower. He was told that, as he was making his final turn, two UFOs appeared on their radar screens. Their paths crossed. This is when he had declared an emergency. The air traffic controllers also told him that there were no other military or civilian aircraft in the area at the time.

A month later, Flight 304 from Acapulco was coming in to land when the pilot had to take evasive action to avoid a catastrophe.

'A big silver object came out of a cloud,' he said. 'It was metallic and circular. We clearly saw the object. It passed directly under the plane and we were forced to make a very difficult manoeuvre to avoid a collision.'

Once safely on the ground, the captain confronted the air traffic controllers. Why had he received no warning, he wanted to know.

There were numerous other events involving UFOs and passenger aircraft, prompting a public outcry. And the Mexican Pilots Association asked Jaime Maussan to present two lectures about the UFOs to their pilots. This is a measure of how worried they were.

'They don't care if they are UFOs or identified flying objects, they just want to avoid an accident,' said Maussan. 'Can you imagine what would happen if there had been a head-on collision with a passenger jet over densely populated Mexico City? How would they explain an accident like this to the general public?'

One puzzle was that, despite the danger posed by UFOs – whether alien or not – appearing along civilian air routes, the Mexican air force has rarely scrambled its fighters to try to intercept them. Perhaps the Mexican government does not regard the UFOs as a threat. Some researchers claim that the government know exactly what the objects are and may even be welcoming them. Whatever the case, the authorities are unwilling to discuss the situation.

Encounters Worldwide

Around August 1984, a flurry of sightings were reported by aircrews over Tasmania, Brazil, France and Russia; doubtless there were many more unreported. Numerous airlines have been involved, but most prefer their pilots not to talk about these encounters for fear of undermining passenger confidence. But no one has yet worked out whether they constitute a physical threat.

On 17 November 1986, at 17:10, Japanese airline pilot Captain Kenju Terauchi, who was flying a 747 cargo plane, saw what he at first thought were lights coming from a military aircraft. During the next half hour, he and his crew realised that things of an unearthly nature had joined them in the skies.

The pilot, first officer and flight engineer saw two lighted structures which were, according to Terauchi, 'about the same size as the body of a DC-8 jet'. It was flying about one thousand feet in front of the cargo plane. Terauchi's radio communications to

27 September 1965: A passenger on an airliner of Nippon Airways took photographs of a lenticular UFO approaching from front rear off the right wingtip and moving faster than the airliner.

Anchorage flight control were strangely garbled, but enough got through that Anchorage urgently contacted a nearby Air Force radar station to see what they were picking up. At various times during the event the UFOs were tracked by the 747 on-board radar and by the USAF ground radar.

As the sky darkened, the UFOs paced the 747 and were finally lost over the distant horizon. Then a pale white light appeared behind the aircraft. Silhouetted against lights on the ground, it looked like an immense, Saturn-shaped object – the size, Terauchi estimated, of 'two aircraft carriers'. He thought it was a 'mother-ship' that had carried the two 'smaller' objects, themselves of no small size. The Anchorage radar was still recording the object's presence. For the first time the crew felt fear. By now the aircraft was running low on fuel, and the captain requested permission to land. The UFO vanished suddenly at 17:39.

Danger Aloft

Another British plane had a close encounter with a huge UFO on 3 February 1999. At around 5:30 p.m. over the North Sea, about sixty miles from the Danish coast, the crew of the Debonair BAel46, a UK-based charter jet flying a party of businessmen from Sweden to the UK, noticed that the plane's underside was immersed in 'incandescent light'. The light lasted for about ten seconds, during which time those on board the plane reported that the jet was buzzed by a 'cylindrical craft' with 'rows of square portholes' . It was 'the size of a battleship'; at least, that is what newspaper reports of the incident said.

Safely on the ground in the UK, the pilot told air traffic control what had happened. They confirmed that there had been no other air traffic in the area. The Debonair's crew filed a near-miss report with the CAA. They were not alone. Three other pilots had independently logged sightings of the UFO. And these could not be dismissed as the misidentification of a terrestrial craft. According to the CAA report, at one point, the UFO was seen to come to an abrupt halt. It then turned westwards and accelerated past the Debonair flight at 'thousands of miles per hour'. And it was no figment of the imagination. As it entered British airspace, it was tracked briefly by military radar.

The Debonair encounter is just one of numerous encounters that took place at the end of the last century. During the 1990s, around fifty such incidents were reported in British airspace alone. Hundreds more have been reported around the world.

Fearing that the UFO in the Debonair encounter might present a danger to other aircraft, Swedish UFOlogist Clas Svahn and British journalist David Clarke investigated. They concluded that, although the Debonair jet had probably encountered an extraterrestrial object, they did not believe it to have been intelligently controlled. Svahn and Clarke noted that there is no mention of a UFO the size of a battleship nor of a craft with rows of portholes in the Debonair crew's near-miss report. That only appeared in the newspapers later. The crew reported only that they had seen an 'unidentified bright light' underneath the aircraft for about ten seconds. Svahn and Clarke pointed out that the crew had not reported seeing a UFO at all, but rather an unidentified aircraft light. And three other pilots who reported the UFO described it simply as a 'flare of light'.

However, the object was tracked for some time by the Debonair's on-board radar. But Svahn and Clarke found this evidence too shot through with holes. The object was only detected some minutes after the visual sighting and it was several miles away. Besides it had been picked up on the plane's weather radar, which was designed to pick up mountains or thunderclouds, not other aircraft. Svahn and Clarke concluded that the radar picked up some surface reflection, unconnected with the UFO.

The nearest radar ground station at Copenhagen had picked up nothing and, although an object was tracked by a UK military radar station, there is some question as to whether it was the same object seen by the Debonair crew. Weighing up the evidence, Svahn and Clarke came to the conclusion that the UFO that buzzed Debonair BAel46 was actually a bright meteor or bolide. Professor Bertil Lindblad, a Swedish expert on these high atmospheric burn-outs, says that, when meteors enter the atmosphere, they disintegrate, producing a trail of ionised gas in their wake and this, in some circumstances, can create the impression of a UFO.

It is often though that most mid-air encounters have natural causes. Although pilots are skilled observers and make good witnesses, there are some things that happen in the sky that are so rare that even an experienced pilot will never have seen one. It is generally believed that the 'foo fighters' reported during World War II, when military pilots saw strange lights in the skies over Europe, were some form of atmospheric phenomenon. They had not been seen before the 1940s because never before in history had thousands of aircraft been in the skies at any one time. Foo fighters are no longer reported; however, small balls of light are often seen which appear to tail aircraft. No satisfactory explanation for these modern-day foo fighters has yet been given, but it is generally assumed that they are some kind of atmospheric or electrical phenomenon that home in on the metal in the same way that a bolt of lightning would.

Collision Course

Although Svahn and Clarke came up with a partial explanation of the Debonair encounter, not all mid-air sightings can be dismissed so easily. In recent years, dozens of aircraft have reported sightings of lozenge-shaped dark brown or black objects in their vicinity. They have been pursued by military fighters, and both commercial pilots and air traffic controllers consider them a threat to life.

On 15 July 1991, a UFO buzzed a Britannia Airways Boeing 737 flying from Crete to London Gatwick, coming within 100 metres of its right wing as it came in to land. In their near-miss report, the crew of the charter flight rated the risk of a collision as 'high'. The 737 was given a comprehensive inspection for possible damage, in case a minor impact had occurred.

According to CAA investigation, the 737 and the UFO had been tracked by Gatwick radar. The unidentified radar blip that crossed the path of the jet streaked away at over 125 miles an hour. All aircraft give off an electronic code signal that identifies them on the radar screen. This object did not, so it was definitely not an aircraft. Gatwick air traffic control were so concerned that they ordered the in-bound jet following the Britannia Airways flight in to land to change course to get it out of the path of the UFO. The unidentified craft then turned south abruptly and disappeared over the English Channel.

After a twelve-month investigation, the CAA concluded that the unidentified flying object was 'probably' a toy balloon. But it is hard to square this theory with the facts. Balloons cannot normally reach altitudes much above 6,000 feet. The UFO was at over 12,000 feet. And balloons certainly cannot travel at 125 miles an hour or change direction abruptly. By coincidence, a weather balloon was released from the nearby town of Crawléy that same evening. The wind took it east, while the UFO was seen flying west and then south. The weather balloon reached a top speed of 45 miles an hour. On the face of it, the 737 narrowly missed a collision with something truly unexplained.

On 24 March 1968, the sixty people flying on the Cork-to-

London shuttle on an Aer Lingus Viscount were not so lucky. Hit by an unknown object, the Viscount plunged into the Irish Sea. No one survived. The air-crash investigation concluded that the Aer Lingus shuttle hit another aircraft. 'The conclusion that there was another aircraft involved is inescapable,' the Irish Inspector of Transport, Richard O'Sullivan, reported in June 1970. But what aircraft? There were none in the area at the time and none were reported missing. However, the air-crash report had ignored the testimony of a number witnesses at Carnsore Point, Ireland, near where the Viscount was lost. They reported seeing a 'dark cigar-like object' in the sky earlier that day.

Another dark, cylindrical object flashed past the cockpit of an Alitalia jet crossing on its descent into London Heathrow in April 1991. It was tracked by radar. On 14 September 1992, a similar craft flew past Australian Airlines Flight 405 over Tasmania. A long, black lozenge crossed the path of a military helicopter near Brignoles, France, on 8 July 1992. And on 9 August 1997, a Swissair Boeing 747 flying from Philadelphia to Zurich encountered a 'long, dark, wingless' cylinder near Boston. The crew reported that it came 'dangerously close'. And these are just the tip of the iceberg. During the 1990s, UFOlogist James Sneddon monitored radio traffic between air crews and air traffic controllers and found that numerous encounters went unreported.

For example, at about 2 a.m. on 1 February 1997 he overheard the following conversation between Gilair 274P, flying from Belfast to Newcastle, and air traffic control:

Gilair: 'Ah, it's... been getting closer in the last sixty seconds. Do you have anything on radar?'
Air Traffic Control: 'Negative. Can you describe the object?'
Gilair: 'Red flamey object.'
Air Traffic Control: 'Ah... I have a primary object [on radar]... range about seven miles. It's more or less stationary.'
Gilair: 'It could be the same one... [it's] stationary, but it got bigger in the last sixty seconds.
Air Traffic Control: 'Okay. Just go left about 30 degrees to

avoid this. It's been steady there [on radar] for the last two three minutes.'

The Gilair aircraft successfully avoided the UFO. When it resumed its normal course for Tyneside, the air traffic controller joked: 'Okay then, fine – that's one for the X Files.'

Details of this incident appeared in no CAA report. According to pilot Graham Shepherd, civil aircrew are asked to keep quiet about sightings for fear of damaging passenger confidence.

Dr Richard Haines of the Ames Research Center in California, who regularly works for NASA, has collated hundreds of reports of mid-air encounters over the past 30 years. He fears that modern aircraft, which rely so heavily on computer systems, are in danger from the electromagnetic fields given off by UFOs.

'Mid-air encounters that threaten lives happen almost every week,' he says, 'but very little money is being spent on them because of the term UFO.'

Shoot 'Em Up

While civilian pilots keep quiet to avoid scaring away passengers, military pilots are bound by oaths of secrecy. However, rather than just taking action to avoid UFOs, they often take them on.

On 16 April 1998, a Draken jet fighter of the Finnish Air Force was on a routine reconnaissance mission over the Russo-Finnish border when the pilot spotted five 'glowing orange objects' flying in formation south-east of Lake Inarijarvi over the frozen tundra. He reported back to the air base at Rovaniemi, 250 miles north of Helsinki.

His commander ordered him to intercept the alien craft. This was easier said than done. He chased them for some time, but was unable to gain on them. Then, when they broke formation, he asked permission to engage them in a dogfight. Granted permission to fire, the pilot locked on, but his weapons systems malfunctioned. The UFOs then regrouped and sped off in a north-easterly direction. The Draken jet turned home. Back at Rovaniemi, all the aircraft's systems were checked and found to be in perfect working order.

One of our Pilots is Missing

Twenty-year-old Australian Frederick Valentich was a keen flyer. He was also a UFO enthusiast and an avid reader on the subject. On 21 October 1978 he decided to fly a hired Cessna 182 over the Bass Strait to King Island from his Melbourne home. That way he could combine his two passions. He knew that, in the previous week, there had been numerous reports of strange cigar-shaped UFOs spotted in the Bass Strait area.

At 6:19 p.m. he took off from Moorabbin Airport in Melbourne in the rented aircraft. He had filed a flight plan for a night flight to King Island over the Bass Strait, which separates the mainland of Australia from Tasmania. He said he was going to collect crayfish for the officers of the local Air Training Corps, and he expected to return to by 10 p.m. that same night.

Valentich was about halfway into his journey when he spotted-something strange over the water. At 7:06 p.m., he contacted Steve Robey, an air traffic controller with the Melbourne Flight Service. 'Is there any known traffic below 5,000 feet?' he asked. Robey said

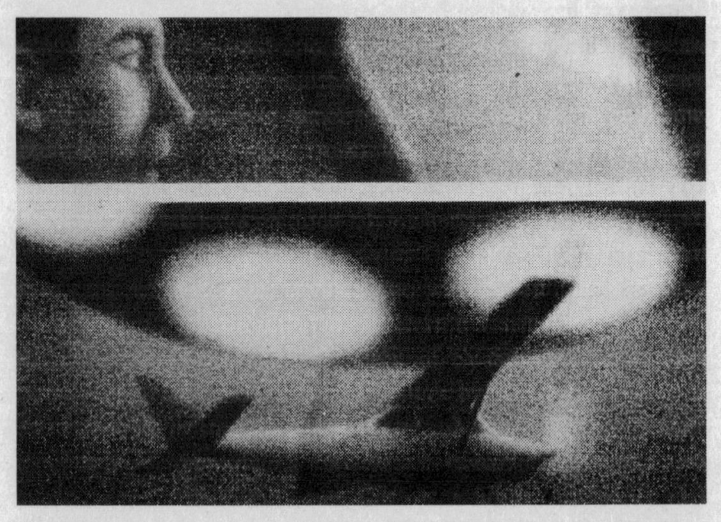

Artwork depicts the possible abduction by UFO of pilot Frederick Valentich, who disappeared over Bass Strait, off Victoria, Australia, on 21 October 1978 and was never seen again.

no other aircraft were expected in that area. The taped conversation following Valentich's query reveal an extraordinary tale:

19.06
Valentich: There seems to be a large aircraft below 5,000.
Robey: What type of aircraft is it?
Valentich: I cannot affirm. It is four bright... it seems to me like landing lights.
19.07
Valentich: The aircraft has just passed over me, at least 1,000 feet above.
Robey: And it is a large aircraft, confirm?
Valentich: Er, unknown due to the speed... Is there any Air Force aircraft in the vicinity?
Robey: No known aircraft.
Valentich: It's approaching now from due east towards me... he's flying over me two, three times at speeds I could not identify...
Robey: Can you describe the, err, aircraft?
Valentich: As it's flying past it's a long shape. Cannot identify more than that, it has such speed...
19.10
Robey: Roger, and how large would the, err, object be?
Valentich: It's got a green light and sort of metallic, like it's all shiny on the outside... It's just vanished.

Valentich then radioed that his engine was 'rough idling'. It was missing and spluttering, but Valentich informed Robey that he would try to reach King Island. Suddenly, sounding extremely distressed, Valentich suddenly reported: 'Ah, Melbourne, That strange craft is hovering on top of me again... hovering and it's not an aircraft!' These were the last words that Robey heard. There was a cry and loud metallic sound before all contact was lost. Valentich never made it to King Island and, from 19:12 on 21 October 1978, the young pilot and his plane were officially declared 'missing'. A full-scale land, air and sea search was launched. It lasted for the next five days, but no trace of Valentich or his Cessna was ever found.

The ensuing official investigation by Australia's Aviation Administration lasted four years. In May 1982, its report was published. The conclusions were hardly worth waiting for. The report merely stated that 'the reason for the disappearance of the aircraft has not been determined'.

In the light of the mysterious circumstances surrounding the disappearance, this left the field wide open for a multitude of theories to be put forward, all attempting to explain Valentich's fate. Naturally, the standard explanation – that, by billion-to-one odds Valentich's Cessna 182 had been hit by space debris – came up. This could easily be discounted: the length of the taped contact between Valentich and Robey ruled it out.

Another theory was that Valentich had become disorientated and had flipped his aircraft over on to its back. In that case, the aircraft he had seen above him would have been his own reflection on the water below. This would also have explained why the engine began misfiring. In that attitude, it would have been starved of fuel. And if he had not righted himself before the engine died, he would have crashed. Again, however, the testimony of Robey, the last man to speak to Valentich, seemed to discount this. Valentich seemed far from disorientated during their conversation. Besides, if he mistook his own reflection in the water for an aircraft above him, what was it he saw below. Valentich's evident coherence during the radio exchange also excluded another possibility – that he was confused and mistook the Cape Otway lighthouse for aviation lights.

The Bass Straits are a route used by drug smugglers to smuggle drugs into Australia. Rumours circulated that Valentich was involved in, or had somehow stumbled into, some criminal venture. But if he was actively involved, how can the conversation with Robey be explained? And if he had just stumbled into it by accident, how can the lights of the craft he saw be explained? Surely drug smugglers would not advertise their activities in this way.

NASA psychologist Dr Richard Haines proposed the theory that Valentich may have fallen foul of a Strategic Defence Initiative programme. He says that, at the time of Valentich's disappearance, the US Defense Intelligence Agency and National Security Agency were using a top-secret facility called Pine Gap in the deserted Australian outback. Haines also claims that these agencies had been performing experiments to test the projection of high-intensity laser beams into the atmosphere, an early stage in the development of a 'Star Wars' weapon.

As incredible as this may sound, Haines' role at NASA gave him access to classified files that are still withheld from the public for 'national security' reasons. What's more, his theory ties in with the Rendlesham forest incident in England. An investigation revealed that the same US intelligence agencies were co-ordinating in the Rendlesham area a similar project to that at Pine Gap.

A more widely accepted theory is that Valentich was a hoaxer. He had just seen the movie *Close Encounters of the Third Kind*, which could have led him to fake his own disappearance. At Moorabbin air field, Valentich had filled the aircraft's fuel tank to capacity and, after his frantic calls to Melbourne, he could have flown on to Tasmania.

The fact that he never turned up in Tasmania has not discouraged proponents of this theory. They say that Valentich may subsequently have lost control of his craft and crashed into the sea. However, no wreckage was found and, once again, Robey, the last man to speak to Valentich, discounts this theory. 'I am convinced in my own mind that he saw something strange,' he said. 'Whether it was a UFO or not I just do not know.'

All these 'logical' explanations for Valentich's disappearance take no account of the events leading up to it. Investigators from the Victorian UFO Research Society (VUFORS) have confirmed that there were numerous reports of flying objects throughout southern Victoria on 21 October 1978, many of them similar to Valentich's. They continued for several days following Valentich's disappearance, then suddenly stopped.

At 2 p.m. on 21 October, the day Valentich vanished, a strange cloud was seen floating in the sky above King Island. Suddenly, a silvery-white object emerged from the cloud. It was said to be about a quarter of the size of the moon. It moved slowly out to the west towards the sea, stopped, then circled back into the cloud.

At 4 p.m., a number of independent witnesses saw two cigar-shaped UFOs, around the size of a jumbo jet, moving west to east across the state of Victoria, towards the Bass Strait. The last sighting was made at around 4:30 p.m. near Cape Otway, though the craft were said to have turned away north and disappeared.

Between 7:06 and 7:12 p.m., at the very time Valentich was having his last conversation with Robey, several people saw a green light over the Bass Strait – at exactly the same time as Valentich was reporting the same thing.

Three minutes later, a witness reported seeing a cigar-shaped arrangement of lights in the sky over the Ormond district of Melbourne. At the same time, two young boys playing with walkie-talkies in Melbourne say they saw a white star-shaped UFO hovering at a low altitude above their heads. The UFO emitted a pulsating hum that seemed to jam their walkie-talkies. Then it disappeared.

The UFOlogists also came up with some photographic evidence. About twenty-one minutes before Valentich disappeared, Melbourne resident Roy Manifold, who was holidaying on King Island, took some photographs. His 35mm camera was mounted on a tripod and set for twenty-second automatic sequencing. It took six shots out over the Bass Strait, two of which show a strange blur out near Cape Otway lighthouse. Although some UFO experts say they show alien craft, the Royal Australian Air Force was not convinced. They say that the photographs show cumulus clouds. However, Australian researcher William H. Spaulding has pointed out that for the clouds to appear within the time sequence of the photographs, they would have to have been travelling at over two hundred miles an hour.

Even so, a UFO encounter only partially explains how Valentich vanished from the face of the earth. Some have suggested that interference from the unidentified craft may have caused the engine failure that he reported in the radio conversation, causing him to crash into the water. If the craft he saw was, indeed, piloted by aliens, the theory goes that they may have 'rescued' Valentich and his Cessna in an emergency airborne abduction. This would explain why no wreckage was found. Alternatively, the plane and its pilot may have simply been lost in the depths of the Bass Strait.

When a young pilot, on his first solo night flight, disappears without trace, the obvious conclusion is 'death by misadventure', but the Valentich case is not as simple as that. Valentich's conversation with air traffic control suggests that he did encounter something that night. Even to this day no one is sure what happened to Frederick Valentich.

Two months later, the UFO activity was reported over New Zealand. On 21 December 1978, Captain John Randle and Captain Vern Powell were flying two Argosy cargo aircraft from Blenheim to Dunedin, in South Island. Both pilots independently reported encountering several UFOs. And there was tangible evidence to back up their sighting. The UFOs had been detected on radar and the contacts confirmed by a number of air traffic controllers.

Astronauts' Sightings

If anyone knows about UFOs it is NASA. After all, NASA is looking out into space, where aliens come from, and it is sending its people out there. And there is little doubt that NASA has much more evidence about extraterrestrials than it is letting on.

Since 1958, when the National Aeronautical and Space Administration was established, NASA astronauts and test pilots have reported having aerial encounters with UFOs and other craft of unknown origin. The first to go public with a sighting was Joseph Walker, who was the pilot of NASA's pioneering space planes, the X-15s. During a speech to the National Conference on the Peaceful Uses of Space Research in May 1962, it was announced that Walker had an aerial encounter with two disc-shaped objects the previous month. And he had filmed them. The following July, Major Robert White, another X-15 pilot, found himself flying in formation with a number of UFOs at 314,000 feet.

NASA pilots are highly trained. But despite these accounts from eminently reliable eyewitness, NASA refused to back its men and

UFOs photographed from spacecraft.

the film and photographs they had shot of these encounters were never released. The official line is that what the two men had seen had been identified as 'flakes of ice'. NASA has also consistently denied having any interest in UFOs. But this is not entirely true. Indeed, a NASA operations manual published in 1967 details the procedures NASA staff must follow when filing UFO sighting reports.

In 1965, the Federal Bureau of Investigation learned from a confidential source that a NASA member of staff was secretly leaking information the space agency had collected on UFOs. The information was being given to two individuals from Pittsburgh who were 'acquainted with the NASA employee' and, to quote the FBI, 'had personal interest in UFOs'.

'The source believes that the information may be classified,' says an FBI report dated 2 September 1965, which was purged of names before being released. 'The source said, for example, that [censored] had seen a motion picture film showing a missile separating and a UFO appearing on the screen. Prior to the flight of Gemini 4, [censored] said to watch out for something interesting because the spaceship had devices aboard to detect UFOs...'

The FBI's reference to a 'motion picture film' held by NASA showing a UFO in flight indicates that NASA does have information on UFOs, which it has kept from the public. The mention of Gemini 4 is particularly intriguing, as one of its astronauts, James McDivitt, has confirmed that he saw some form of unidentified flying object during that flight. McDivitt does not believe that the object was alien in origin, but he disagrees with the theory UFO sceptic James Oberg put forward, that the object he saw was merely the second stage of Gemini 4's Titan rocket. 'If this is the case, the only puzzle remaining is McDivitt's apparent failure to recognise his own rocket,' wrote UFO researcher Timothy Good in his 1996 book, *Beyond Top Secret*.

On Gemini 12, Edwin 'Buzz' Aldrin, later the second man to set foot on the Moon, photographed three glowing orbs. The fifteen shots he took in a three-minute period show clearly that the objects were moving at some speed. Both Aldrin and NASA deny they were of alien origin.

When, in May 1961, President Kennedy promised to put a man on the Moon 'before the decade is out', NASA went into overdrive. To achieve Kennedy's goal, an American spacecraft would have to leave Earth orbit, cosmologically our own back yard. It then would have to cross a quarter-of-a-million miles of hostile interplanetary space and land on an alien world. NASA scientists must have at least considered the possibility that its astronauts might encounter extraterrestrials. And when the astronauts of Apollo 11 finally took their first tentative steps on the surface of the Moon on 20 July 1969, no one – not even the most hardened sceptic – could have entirely discounted the possibility that they might meet some form of alien life.

As well as being a technical achievement, the Moon landings

were a highly organised exercise in public relations. Even the words uttered by Neil Armstrong when he descended on to the lunar surface were written for him – though, in the event, he got them wrong. He should have said: 'That's one small step for a man, one giant leap for mankind.' Not: 'That's one small step for man, one giant leap for mankind,' which does not make sense. Otherwise, the astronauts were word perfect. At the press conferences when they returned they said that nothing unusual occurred, and Armstrong stated categorically: 'There were no objects reported, found, or seen on Apollo 11 or any other Apollo flight other than of natural origin.'

However, rumours soon circulated that, during their stay on the Moon's surface, the astronauts were never alone. On one occasion the following conversation took place between the Apollo 11 crew and Mission Control:

> Apollo 11: What was it? What the hell was it? That's all I want to know. These babies were huge, sir... Oh, God, you wouldn't believe it...
> NASA: What... What the hell's going on?
> Apollo 11: They're here, under the surface.
> NASA: What's there? Mission Control calling Apollo 11.
> Apollo 11: Roger, we're here, all three of us. But we've found some visitors... They've been here for quite a while judging by the installations... I'm telling you there are other spacecraft out there. They're lined up in ranks on the far side of the crater edge...

This exchange was not broadcast and the tapes and transcripts were classified. But a former NASA employee, Otto Binder, claimed that the conversation was overheard by amateur radio enthusiasts eavesdropping on a confidential channel reserved for high security messages. Timothy Good believes that Neil Armstrong and Buzz Aldrin saw aliens on the Moon, but he says that this secret conversation between Mission Control and Apollo 11 astronauts was actually monitored by Soviet scientists. Russian physicist and Professor of Mathematics Dr Vladimir Azhazha said that the encounter occurred shortly after the lunar module landed, but that the astronauts' report was never heard by the public because NASA censored it.

Corroboration of this story came from a NASA communications expert Maurice Chatelain, who helped design the Apollo spacecraft and worked for NASA at the time. He stated publicly that the Apollo 11 encounter with the UFOs was 'common knowledge in NASA' and that all the Apollo missions had been observed by UFOs. In an interview given in 1979, Chatelain confirmed that NASA had built a time delay in the transmissions between Apollo 11 and Mission Control so that any information regarding extraterrestrial 'visitors' could be censored.

Photographs of the Apollo 12 mission released by NASA show anomalous streaks of light over the surface of the Moon. One photograph of a moonwalk, some UFO enthusiasts say, has been cropped to cut out a brightly lit alien craft hovering over an astronaut's head. The Apollo 12 command module Yankee Clipper photographed a bright disc that, on enlargement, was full of intricate detail. Another glowing disc was photographed from command module Odyssey during the ill-fated Apollo 13 mission. Other pictures from that mission showed anomalous streaks of light, a red cigar-shaped object and other foreign bodies in the skies. And as the Apollo 14's lunar module Antares flew over the craters Lansberg C and A, 'a large lighted object with windows swept into view'. NASA has refused to comment.

Chatelain said that from the beginning of the manned space programme astronauts had been given code words to use so, if they saw alien craft, they could talk about them over the airwaves. 'Walter Schirra aboard Mercury 8 was the first the astronauts to use the code name "Santa Claus" to indicate a flying saucer,' Chatelain said.

He also claimed that: 'All Apollo and Gemini flights were followed at a distance, and sometimes quite closely, by space vehicles of extraterrestrial origin. Every time it occurred, the astronauts informed Mission Control who then ordered absolute silence.'

This was confirmed by Mercury 7 astronaut Scott Carpenter, who said: 'At no time, when the astronauts were in space, were they alone; there was constant surveillance by UFOs.'

Chatelain said that UFO encounters were common knowledge at NASA, though no one ever talked about them. He believed that some of the alien craft originated on Titan, a moon of Saturn, pointing out that at on a least one occasion in the 1970s, when a NASA probe neared Titan, its photographic and radio equipment malfunctioned. NASA, Chatelain said, is involved in a conspiracy of silence.

NASA denied censoring Apollo 11's transmissions and scorn was poured on Binder and Chatelain, despite their outstanding credentials. Another NASA employee with impeccable credentials is Apollo 14's lunar module pilot, Edgar Dean Mitchell, who spent thirty-three hours walking on the surface of the Moon. He believes that UFO encounters are real and that there is a cover-up.

'I am convinced there is a small body of valid information,' he said, 'and that there is a body of information ten times as big that is total disinformation that is put out by the source to confuse the whole issue. The information is now held primarily by a body of semi- or quasi-private organisations that have kind of spun off from military intelligence organisations of the past...

'The danger is that they are still operating under a black budget, which has been estimated at over $30 billion a year. And nobody knows what goes into black budgets. The prime requisite is security first and everything else second... I would say, however, that if there was knowledge of extraterrestrial contact existing in the government, and we were sent out into space blind and dumb to such information, I think it is a case of criminal culpability. To send us up there into a what-if scenario? If the evidence is real, and we were led to believe that no such thing was possible – to me, that's criminal.'

He is backed by astronaut Colonel Gordon Cooper, who had once held the record for the longest spacc fight – thirty-four hours – and was one of the first Americans to orbit the Earth. In 1985, Cooper appeared before a United Nations panel chaired by

Secretary General Kurt Waldheim and told them what he knew.

'I believe that extraterrestrial vehicles and their crews are visiting this planet from other planets, which are a little more technically advanced than we are on Earth,' said Cooper. 'I feel that we need to have a top-level programme to scientifically collect and analyse data concerning any type of encounter, and to determine how best to interfere with these visitors in a friendly fashion.'

Cooper claimed that he had not only 'been into the fringes of the vast areas of which "they" travel,' but also, 'I did have occasion in 1951 to have two days of observation of many flights of "them", of different sizes flying in fighter formation... they were at a higher altitude than we could reach.'

Aliens continue to observe man's puny attempts that space flight. Around 6:30 a.m. on 14 March 1990, Donald Ratsch, amateur radio enthusiast from Baltimore, Maryland, was monitoring the radio transmissions from Discovery when he heard the pilot say: 'Houston, Discovery, we have a problem. We have a fire.' Shortly after, Rasch claims an additional transmission was heard: 'Houston, this is Discovery. We still have the alien spacecraft under observance.'

However, NASA mission specialist Bob Oeschler, a former mission specialist with NASA, investigated and discovered that the second message did not come from the Shuttle at all. Instead, he says that the signal came from Fort Meade, Maryland – not far from Baltimore. Fort Meade is the home to America's National Security Agency, which has a longstanding involvement in UFO reports. Oeschler's conclusion was that the broadcast was 'an institutionally orchestrated hoax for subtle intelligence purpose'.

Oeschler was later informed by a senior NASA source that the Shuttle had indeed encountered a UFO around that time. The encounter, he was told, lasted for eight hours, and caused a major disruption of Discovery's electrical systems. It seems that NASA does indeed know about UFO and alien encounters. It is just not saying.

Sightings from the Past

Anomalous Airships

There is nothing new about UFOs. They have been seen throughout human history. Sightings of mysterious lights in the skies began long before the phrase 'flying saucer' was coined in 1947, when the idea caught on that flying objects may be craft from distant planets flown by aliens.

In ancient times, UFOs were thought to be flying chariots or some other sign of a heavenly presence. But in the nineteenth century, with the onset of the airship, it was conceded that UFOs might have earthly origins. Even today, many sightings spring from human activity in the air, but some early reports offer a tantalising taste of the mystery that was to come.

An illustration of an airship from the *Chicago Times-Herald*, 12 April 1897.

The first modern-day UFO 'flap' occurred in North America as the nineteenth century ended. In 1896 and 1897, there were numerous reports of 'airships' across the US and the prairies of Canada, even though, at that time, no airship had crossed the Atlantic. Between 6 and 7 p.m. on 17 November 1896, an intensely bright light, like an 'electric arc lamp', was seen moving over the housetops in Sacramento, California. Some of the hundreds of eyewitnesses claimed to have got a closer view of the craft. They said that it was an enormous, cigar-shaped object, apparently made of aluminium, held aloft by large wings. It was assumed to be one of the newfangled airships; a couple of witnesses said they heard a voice calling down, saying: 'We hope to be in San Francisco by tomorrow noon!'

An airship over Oakland, California, in 1896 (from *San Francisco Call*, November 1896).

In the following January, the *Omaha Bee* carried reports of a series of mysterious sightings in Hastings, Nebraska. 'Several Hastings people report that an airship, or something of the kind, has been sailing around in the air west of this city,' the papers reported. 'It was first noticed sometime last fall when it was seen floating in the air about five hundred feet above the ground, and, after standing still for about thirty minutes, it began to circle about and took a northerly direction for about two miles, after which it returned to its starting place and sank into oblivion.

'At first sight it had the appearance of an immense star, but after closer observation the powerful light shows [itself] by its color to be artificial. It certainly must be illuminated by powerful electric dynamos for the light sent forth by it is wonderful. At 9:30 last Monday night [25 January 1897], the large glaring light was seen to circle around for a few minutes and then descend for about two hundred feet, circling as it travelled at a remarkable speed... A close watch is being kept for its reappearance.'

In April, an 'airship' began making regular visits to Kansas. News spread east. On 2 April 1897, the *Evening Times* of Pawtucket, Rhode Island, carried a story saying: 'The mysterious airship seen often in Kansas during the past two weeks was seen again last night at Everest, Brown County, in the north-western part of the state... The ship was seemingly erratic in its movements. Instead of moving in a straight line, it rode up and down, now to the left, and again to the right, but always, apparently, under

Mystery airship seen over Sacramento, California, in 1896, as depicted in the *San Francisco Call*.

absolute control... when the ship has been seen, it has come from the north in the early evening and returned in the early morning. In all expectation that this programme will be repeated, a good number of the citizens of Everest will remain out all night, hoping for another glance at the mysterious visitor.'

In May 1897, the plague of airships seems to have moved northwards and new sightings began to come in from the other side of the Canadian border in Manitoba and British Columbia. These peaked in July and August. For example, on 14 August 1897, the *Vancouver Daily World* asked: 'Have you seen the light in the heavens? If not, you are not up to date. It has been hovering in the skies above Vancouver almost every night this week, and has been

Mystery airship seen over Sacramento, California, in 1896, as depicted in the *San Francisco Call*.

viewed by many. It was last seen on Friday evening and may be on view tonight, and again it may not. Last night the strange object in the skies was noticed to the north of the city... travelling in an easterly direction. The luminous ball of fire, or airship as some call it, was closely watched. It approached with great swiftness, paused in mid-air, then surrounded itself with flashes of colour and moved towards the north-east. At times it looked like a ball of fire, at others it had a dull lustre and small particles of fire would shoot from the great glowing mass.'

Perhaps some unknown American inventor had developed an airship independently. But why did all trace of him, and them, disappear after 1897?

Phantom Fliers

With the turn of the new century, UFOs seemed to turn their attention elsewhere. The earliest known UFO picture was taken over the Norwegian town of Drobach in 1907. The photograph is hazy, but the object is saucer shaped and could not be mistaken for the airships of the day.

A large numbers of cases have been documented in eastern Europe, though witnesses often interpreted them as if they were from an earlier age. This one, dating from 1904, is typical: 'In Romania's Transylvania a farmer was still in his fields with his cart long after midnight. Suddenly he saw a fiery wheel over the Muntii Apuseni [mountains], coming down to the ground. The wheel approached fast, turning as it did so, and the farmer stood by helplessly. When the fiery wheel was quite close to him it changed into the shape of a human being, who looked at the farmer for a long time without speaking.'

Meanwhile, back in the States, the sightings had started again. On 1 February 1908, a reddish cigar-shaped object was seen flying over the town of Kent in Washington state, between 7:00 and 9:00 in the evening. One witness described it as 'two or three times as bright as Jupiter'. The same object appeared again the next night. After that, it was never seen again.

New Zealand UFOlogist Murray Bott unearthed a wave of sight-

Possibly the earliest photograph of a UFO, taken 27 July 1907 over Drobach, Norway. The lens-like object was photographed over the harbour anchorage two clippers can be seen at anchor.

ings the following year down under. On 27 July 1909, the Clutha Leader of Balclutha on New Zealand's South Island reported that 'some half dozen boys were playing on the beach at Kaka Point [when they] saw a huge illuminated object moving about in the air. It appeared as if it was going to alight at Kaka Point... The boys thought it was being attracted by their lantern and left it on the beach. The airship then glided around the rocks at the old pilot station and nearly came in contact with them. It shortly afterwards disappeared. The boys said it was as big as a house.'

Another encounter had taken place at Kelso on South Island just four days early. That time: 'A small group of schoolchildren and some residents reported that an airship came down and bobbed around in the sky over the school for a few minutes.' A reporter for the *Otago Daily Times* went to Kelso and interviewed the witnesses. 'All those scholars who saw the ship were interrogated singly and independently [and] were asked to draw an impression of what they had seen... The result was six drawings, the degree of resemblance and unanimity of which was nothing short of dumbfounding to all sceptics.'

Drawing of airship seen by P. C. Kettle over Peterborough, 23 March 1909.

Meanwhile, on the other side of the world, the 21 May 1909 edition of the *East Anglian Daily Times* carried the headline: 'Britain Invaded!' Its subheadings said: 'Airships in East Anglia, Wales, and Midlands. Phantom Fleet. Norwich and Southend Paid A Visit.' The body of the story reported: 'The airship fleet which is invading England had a busy night on Wednesday. We speak of a fleet because, according to correspondents, there must be not only one, but half a dozen mysterious cigar-shaped machines with quivering lights and whirring mechanisms flitting about the country by night. Wednesday night's observers report manifestations at such widely divergent points as: Southend-on-Sea, Birmingham, Norwich, Tasburgh, Wroxham and Pontypool.'

In the run-up to World War I another wave of airship sightings took place over western Europe. As the belligerents were eyeing each other up, it was assumed that the reports of unidentified flying were sightings of experimental enemy military machines.

In 1912, there was an epidemic of sightings in Britain. Questions were asked in the House of Commons and Winston Churchill, then First Lord of the Admiralty, issued a statement that an unidentified flying object had been seen on the night of 27 November 1912. Flares had been lit at the airfield at Eastchurch in anticipation of an aircraft landing. But nothing had descended from the sky. This was the first of a number of so-called 'scareships'. In January 1913, there were scareship sightings over Cardiff, Liverpool, Dover and Yorkshire. Witnesses said that the craft travelled very fast and left a cloud of smoke in their wake. One, according to a witness, circled, 'as if surveying something'. To this day, there has been no satisfactory explanation of these sightings.

Also in 1913, in Moravia –which was then part of the Austro-Hungarian Empire, but now in the Czech Republic – it was reported that: 'A 20 year-old boy was travelling from Brno to Zidence in clear weather at the end of the summer. Between 21:00 and 22:00 hours he saw six objects very high in the sky, like large fiery red stars, travelling soundlessly round a fixed point in a clockwise direction.'

UFOs also returned to North America that year. In 1913, a mysterious procession of glowing lights was seen by hundreds of witnesses above Saskatchewan. By this time the vogue for airships was waning and they were described as 'ghost aeroplanes'.

UFO sightings dropped off during the Great War, presumably because people were concentrating on what was going on on the ground. But wartime Europe did record the first occasion when an aircraft fired on a UFO. It occurred on 31 January 1916. The official record of the encounter says: 'At 20:45 hours, local time near Rochford, England, Flight Sublieutenant J.E. Morgan, flying at 5,000 feet saw a row of lights like lighted windows on a railway carriage with the blinds drawn. Thinking it was a German Zeppelin, he fired his Webley Scott pistol. The light rose and rapidly disappeared.'

Following the war, with more aircraft aloft, sightings became more common. In the 1960s Francis (later Sir Francis) Chichester was a renowned single-handed yachtsman, but in 1931 he made the first east-west flight across the Tasman Sea from New Zealand to Australia in a Gypsy Moth biplane fitted with floats. On 10 June 1931, during the flight, he saw a 'flashing airship' and reported the incident in his book *The Lonely Sea and the Sky*, first published in 1932.

The following year, Lieutenant Tage Anderson and Lieutenant Peter Grunnet of the Royal Danish Air Force found that their plane was being tailed by a UFO off the coast of Greenland.

'It was nothing like the flying machines of that period,' said Grunnet. 'It was hexagonal, flat and seemingly made of aluminium or some other metal, with no breaks in the surface and no rivets. At the time, I had a spooky feeling. I can't explain it. It was as if I "felt" the presence of whoever was inside that craft and the feeling was hostile.'

Suddenly the whole of Scandinavia was swamped with sightings of 'ghost planes'. Witnesses said they had multiple engines and out-performed any known aircraft. They were flown by mysterious pilots wearing what looked like goggles.

Foo Fighters

Late in 1941 the Chiefs of the Imperial General Staff began to fear that the Nazis had developed a secret weapon. RAF aircrew had reported numerous unexplained sightings in the skies. Michael Bentine – who later found fame as one of the Goons – was an RAF Intelligence Officer during World War II. He debriefed Polish bomber crews who said they had seen a strange 'weapon' that flew

Foo fighters in the middle of a formation of Tachikawa KI-36 reconnaissance aircraft over Suzuka mountain range, central Japan, 1942.

alongside their aircraft. Others would report strange lights that hovered close to their aircraft, often too close for comfort. Sometimes these lights would flash across the sky at tremendous speeds. They did not attack the aircraft directly, but they often disrupted the electrical equipment on board. Although the name had not yet been coined, they acted in the same way as what we call 'flying saucers'.

These lights were not seen only in Europe, nor exclusively from the air. One evening in September 1941, the SS *Pulaski*, an old Polish vessel that was being used as a British troop carrier, was steaming across the Indian Ocean when seaman Mar Doroba looked up and saw 'a strange globe glowing with greenish light, about half the size of the full moon'. Doroba estimated that the object was flying at an altitude of approximately 4,500 feet. It appeared to follow the ship for the next hour.

On 26 February 1942, seaman William J. Methorst made a similar sighting from a ship in the Timor Sea, off northern Australia. In 1957 he told Australia's Victorian Flying Saucer Society: 'While

UFO photographed over Tientsien, Hopeh, China, in 1941.

on watch for enemy aircraft just after noon, I was scanning the skies with binoculars when suddenly I saw a large illuminated disc approaching at terrific speed. After reporting it to the officers on the bridge, they were unable to identify it as any known aircraft. After keeping track of this object for about three to four hours, as it flew in big circles and at the same height, the craft suddenly veered off in a tremendous burst of speed and disappeared from sight.'

The logical explanation was that these sightings were an electrical phenomenon related to St Elmo's Fire, the glowing that occurs around a ship's masts or an aircraft's wings due to a build-up of static electricity. But as more reports came in, military intelligence began to fear that the Germans or Japanese might even have developed this effect into a weapon. When the attack on Pearl Harbor in December 1941 brought America into the war, United States Air Force pilots began to see these strange unidentified flying objects too, and they nicknamed them 'phantoms' or 'foo fighters', after one of the comic sayings of the popular cartoon character Smokey

Stover. They were also seen from the ground. US Marine Sergeant Stephen J. Brickner saw a whole wing of them.

'The sightings occurred on August 12, 1942, at about ten in the morning while I was with my squad on the island of Tulagi in the southern Solomons, west of Guadalcanal,' he reported. 'It was a bright tropical morning with high banks of white, fleecy clouds. I was cleaning my rifle on the edge of my foxhole, when suddenly the air raid warning was sounded. I immediately slid into my foxhole, with my back to the ground and my face turned up to the sky. I heard the formation before I saw it. Even then, I was puzzled by the sound. It was a mighty roar that seemed to echo in the heavens. It didn't sound at all like the "sewing machine" drone of the Jap formations. A few seconds later, I saw the formation of silvery objects directly overhead.

'They were flying very high above the clouds... the formation was huge, I would say over 150 objects were in it... this formation was in straight lines of ten or twelve objects, one behind the other. The speed was a little faster than Jap planes, and they were soon

World War II foo fighters.

out of sight. A few other things puzzled me: I couldn't seem to make out any wings or tails. They seemed to wobble slightly, and every time they wobbled they would shimmer brightly from the sun. Their colour was like highly polished silver. All in all, it was the most awe-inspiring and yet frightening spectacle I have seen in my life.'

But despite numerous sightings of foo fighters by both British and American pilots, over Europe and the Pacific, no one could decide whether they were natural or man-made or whether they were dangerous. Nor had anyone devised a counter-measure.

By 1943, the British had become so concerned about the potential threat of foo fighters that they set up a special study group. According to the official record, it was headed by a Lieutenant General Massey. However, there is no other mention of a General Massey in the military records. Nevertheless the Massey Project collected hundreds of first-hand accounts of encounters with foo fighters over the next few years.

One of the reports, from a C.J.J., was found buried in the files of British and American intelligence. (During World War II, documents were copied and shared.) He was a nose gunner with an anti-submarine squadron. This wing were patrolling over the Bay of Biscay one day in November 1942 when the tail gunner reported they were being followed. A 'massive' wingless object had suddenly appeared behind the bomber. C.J.J. climbed out of his nose turret to take a look. The whole crew saw it and C.J.J. examined it at close quarters from the waist gunners' position. It followed them for about fifteen minutes, before making an abrupt 180-degree turn and disappearing. Meanwhile another one of the bomber's crew, a Sergeant M.F.B., was busy photographing it with his K-20 camera. C.J.J. said that only one of the pictures came out, but it was a 'perfect print'. It has yet to surface.

Most witnesses reported shapeless lights. They appeared to lack any clearly designed form or substance. Also, the objects rarely showed up on radar. However, another photograph was taken of three UFOs following a US bomber over the Sea of Japan in 1943.

It seems that the foo fighters did not like this attention. Towards the end of 1943, all sightings of them mysteriously halted, but the following year they were back with a vengeance. From April 1944 to August 1945, reports of hundreds of sightings of foo fighters came in from around the world. When American troops hit Omaha beach on the morning of 6 June as part of the Normandy landings, a dark, cigar-shaped object was seen crossing the horizon by hundreds of witnesses. When the Allies reached Germany in 1945, thirty Allied soldiers in Darmstadt watched six or seven bright yellow-orange circular objects approach the autobahn from the west at an altitude of about 140 feet. Over Tawara, Japan, a 'bogey' blip on a radar screen was calculated to be moving at the incredible speed of 690 miles an hour, at a time when planes had yet to break the sound barrier. With the fall of Japan, the Allies occupied the country, and American and Japanese soldiers saw objects described as 'round, speedy balls of fire' streaking over Tokyo.

Serviceman Leonard H. Stringfield was on board an American C-46 plane on his way to Tokyo as part of the Allied occupation force on 28 August 1945. The plane was midway between the Pacific islands of Ie Shoma and Iwo Jima when an engine began to fail.

Stringfield recalled: 'As the plane dipped, sputtered oil, and lost altitude, I remember looking out through one of the windows and, to my surprise, seeing three unidentifiable blobs of brilliant white light, each about the size of a dime held at arm's length. The lights travelled in a straight line through the clouds, keeping pace and staying parallel with the C-46. When my plane pulled up the objects remained below and then disappeared into a cloudbank.'

Years later, when Stringfield became a prominent UFOlogist, he came across cases in which UFOs seemed to be responsible for electromagnetic disturbances in cars and planes. It was only then that he connected the C-46's sputtering engine with the anomalous blobs. He also recalled that it was the port engine that had failed and the UFOs had been on the port side of the plane. So the foo fighters were no secret weapon. The war was over, following the Japanese surrender on 10 August, two more weeks before Stringfield's sighting.

During the war, information about foo fighters was top secret. But with the war over, the truth could be told. In December 1945 *American Legion Magazine* published an article on the phenomenon. The author concluded that: 'the foo fighter mystery continues unsolved... and your guess as to what they were is as good as mine, for nobody really knows.' That is as true today as it was then.

The foo fighters turned up again during the Korean War. And, although they have changed their name with succeeding generations, they are still seen today. After the war they became known as 'ghost rockets', then 'flying saucers'. Now they are called UFOs and there are reasons to believe they are of alien origin.

Fireballs

It was only after the end of World War II that the Allies discovered that the Germans were indeed developing a revolutionary, top-secret weapons called the *Feuerball*, or 'fireball', which could have been mistaken for a foo fighter. According to researcher Dr Renato Vesco, a flat, circular flying machine powered by a special turbojet engine was developed by scientists at the aeronautical establishment in Wiener Neustadt and actually saw action towards the end of the war. Vesco also claims that the principles of the *Feuerball* were used to develop a larger supersonic craft called the *Kugelblitz*, or 'ball lightning fighter'. Built in the underground factories at Kahla, in Thuringia, central Germany, it took to the air in February 1945, three months before the fall of the Third Reich.

In 1975, when the papers of the deceased World War II Luftwaffe officer Rudolph Schriever were being sorted, they were found to contain the design of a large flying saucer, including numerous sketches and copious notes. Schriever's friends said that, up until his death, he claimed that post-war UFO sightings proved that his work had been taken seriously.

However, the Germans themselves were plagued by the foo fighters. In 1944, the German Wehrmacht set up an office to investigate sighting reports of anomalous flying objects. The Luftwaffe's Sonderburo ('Special Office') 13 went about its task thoroughly until it was shut down when Germany was overrun in

A dark sphere (UFO?) following bombers over the Japan Sea, 1943.

April 1945. Although it was only in operation for a matter of months, Sonderburo 13 collected a vast amount of information.

The first sighting the Sonderburo studied came from a pilot called Hauptmann (Captain) Fischer. At 17:35 on 14 March 1942, Fischer was scrambled to investigate a strange blip on the radar of a secret air base in Banak, Norway. He intercepted the intruder at 10,000 feet and radioed a description back to base. What he could see, he said, was an 'aerial whale'. It was an enormous, streamlined craft around 90 metres long and 15 metres in diameter. This description sounds like a Zeppelin, but it was not. The craft, Fischer said, stayed horizontal for several seconds, then stood on end and soared away vertically at great speed.

Then, at 10:45 on the morning of 29 September 1944, a new Messerschmitt ME-262 Schwalbe jet was being put through its paces when the test pilot spotted two luminous points of light to starboard. He banked right at full speed and found himself face-to-face with a cylindrical craft about a hundred feet long. It had openings along its side and a long antenna at the front. Again, the description would have fitted an airship, but the pilot saw it take off

Ludvig Lindback, brother to the principle witness, Knut, at Lake Kolmjarv, site of the 19 July 1946 rocket/UFO crash in Sweden.

at a speed of over 1,250 miles an hour.

Ghost Rockets

The division of Europe into Soviet and Western spheres of influence in 1945 and the beginnings of the Cold War meant that the military on both sides of the Iron Curtain were constantly on the alert for signs of open hostility. Following the use of V2 rockets by the Nazis and the development of the atomic bomb by the Allies, the stakes were now that much higher.

Everyone, it seemed, was afraid of the V1s and V2s that had devastated London only two years before. Both sides had seized German scientists who had built the V2, and they dedicated themselves to developing bigger and more long-range missiles that could carry nuclear warheads. The race to construct intercontinental ballistic missiles was on, and both sides were terrified that the other might get there first. Everyone's eyes were on the skies.

In the summer of 1946, just a year after the end of the war in Europe, mysterious missiles were sighted in the skies over Western Europe. They were first seen over Finland, Norway, Sweden and

Denmark. Similar reports came in from Portugal, Italy and Greece, then from India and North Africa. Reports of sightings – many from reliable sources – talked of wingless, silver objects in the sky. Often they had a flame at the tail, and a trail of smoke. A frontline country in the Cold War, Sweden took these reports very seriously. In July 1946, the authorities there set up a committee of investigation, comprising leading scientists and engineers and representatives from the armed forces. An appeal for sightings brought a deluge of reports. When the mundane and easily explicable were winnowed out, the committee began investing those that exhibited what it termed 'high strangeness' – for example, unidentified flying objects that were estimated to be travelling at many thousands of miles an hour. It was, of course, only in October 1947 that Chuck Yeager broke the sound barrier in a Bell X-1 experimental rocket plane that topped six hundred miles an hour.

In Sweden these identified flying objects became known as 'ghost rockets', after the 'ghost planes' seen over Scandinavia in the 1930s. The fear was that the new rockets, along the lines of V2s, had been developed by the Soviet Union and that they were straying or being fired deliberately into Swedish airspace from test sites inside the USSR.

When the Swedish government took the matter up in Moscow, the Soviet authorities denied all knowledge of the ghost rockets. But this denial was taken with a pinch of salt. No one really believed what the Soviets said. Clearly the Soviet Union was developing rocket-powered weapons, but why they would test them near the Scandinavian border rather than out in the broad plains of Siberia was a mystery. Nevertheless the Swedish sightings became news world-wide. Even the Prime Minister of South Africa, Jan Smuts, warned in a radio broadcast of the threat the Soviet rockets presented.

Russian rockets were of particular interest to the US. One of the staff of the US embassy in Stockholm saw a mystery rocket, and ghost rockets were a regular feature of the diplomatic traffic between the Swedish legation and the State Department at the time.

Karl-Gosta Bartoll investigating the bottom of Lake Kolmjarv, Sweden.

'My own source is personally convinced that some foreign power is experimenting over Sweden,' says one State Department memo of 1946, 'and he guesses it is Russia.'

The Pentagon became so concerned that it sent a Lieutenant General from the US 14th Army Air Force and General David Sarnoff from military intelligence to Sweden. Sarnoff was an expert on aerial warfare and he concluded that the ghost rockets seen over Norway and Sweden were 'real missiles'.

British radar experts were also despatched to Stockholm. Their reports were sent back to the director of Air Defence Intelligence, the legendary R.V. Jones. A scientist by training, Jones was known as the Sherlock Holmes of the War Office. During World War II, he had laboriously pieced together decoded German communications, air reconnaissance photographs and information gleaned from Allied spies, to work out what the enemy was up to. From the beginning of the Swedish flap, he doubted that the ghost rockets were coming from the Soviet Union. It made no sense. The USSR had vast tracts of lands to the east where it could test secret weapons. Why risk launching them where they could fly into the airspace of another – albeit neutral – country, where they would inevitably fall into the hands of the enemy?

And if these were test flights, how could they be carried out with so few mishaps? When testing the V2, Nazi scientists had experienced a failure rate of ten per cent. Assuming a failure rate a tenth of that, Jones argued that several ghost rockets would have crashed on Swedish territory. Yet none had been recovered. Nevertheless, the British authorities continued to take the sightings very seriously. One of Jones's colleagues in Air Defence Intelligence analysed a series of reports in which a similar object had been seen by several observers in widely separated parts of Sweden within a few minutes of each other. It seemed reasonable to assume that they had all seen the same object and, from the times of the sightings, the officer calculated that the object had zigzagged across southern Sweden, travelling at up to 2,000 miles an hour.

Jones rejected this theory. He agree that it was likely that all the observers had seen the same object, but he noticed that they had all seen it in the sky to the east. This would make sense only if the object was at a much greater height and distance than they had

Ghost rocket at Lake Kolmjarv, Sweden, 1946. On 29 July 1946 men from the engineer troops started to build a raft to be used to investigate the lake. A machine for detecting metal was placed on the raft.

realised. In that case, what they were seeing was probably a daylight meteor or bolide. However, Jones's colleague point out that, if the object was a bolide high in the sky, all the witnesses would have seen the object at exactly the same time. But the sightings were spread over several minutes. Jones said there was no great mystery to why the witnesses had reported seeing the object a few minutes apart. Few people kept their watches set to exactly the right time, and besides, the witnesses would not necessarily have looked at their watches directly after they saw the object.

It seemed clear that progress could only be made if the investigators got their hands on a ghost rocket, or at least part of one. Then a report that a rocket had crashed into Lake Kolmjarv in Sweden came in. But when the crash was investigated, it could not be verified and, despite enormous effort, no debris was recovered. On another occasion, half a dozen irregularly shaped lumps of material, supposedly ejected from a ghost rocket in flight, were obtained. They were shipped to Jones in London, who forwarded them to the Chemical Analysis Section at Farnborough.

The next day a senior chemist telephoned him in a state of excitement. Analysis, he said, had revealed an unknown chemical in one of the samples. Jones was mystified. He telephoned the chief of the chemical laboratory and questioned him. It turned out that the chemists had been analysing the samples for metal and other minerals. If the ghost rocket was man-made it would almost certainly have been made out of metal, while meteorites are either stone or iron. However, Jones knew that some rarer types of meteorite contain a significant amount of carbon.

'No one had stopped to look at the material in an effort to get the analysis made quickly, and they had failed to test for carbon,' said Jones. When he pointed this out 'there was a gasp from the other end of the telephone as the penny dropped.'

As the ghost rockets seemed to have an innocent explanation, in August 1946, the Norwegian authorities instructed their newspapers not to report any more sightings. However, the Swedes went on looking, though the government banned any mention of the location where the rockets had been seen in case it was used by the

Ghost rocket at Lake Kolmjarv, Sweden, 1946. between 20 July and 9 August more than 35,000 samples were taken from the bottom of the lake from two rafts. The electrical mining apparatus that was used at the start did not get any readings.

rocket-builders to tell how accurate or otherwise their launches had been.

Meanwhile, the Swedish investigating committee continued to sift through the reported sightings, separating those that could be explained as weather balloons, misidentified aircraft, meteors, clouds, etc., from those of 'high strangeness'. In October 1946, the committee reported that, of some one thousand sightings, around 80 per cent had mundane causes. The remaining 20 per cent 'cannot be the phenomena of nature or products of the imagination, nor can [they] be referred to as Swedish aeroplanes,' the report said.

In their report, the investigators also said that, although they could not prove that the ghost rockets were not Soviet-built rockets, they thought it was unlikely. After this rather inconclusive end, reports of ghost rockets tailed off. The following year, the first 'flying saucers' were seen. But were these just ghost rockets or foo fighters under another name?

Spitzbergen

Even though interest in ghost rockets soon faded, especially after the firsts sightings of 'flying saucers' in America in 1947, Scandinavia continued to be a target for anomalous objects – and one may even have been captured. In June 1952, stories were beginning to come out in the German press about an alleged UFO crash on the island of Spitzbergen, off the northern coast of Norway.

The stories reported that six Norwegian jets were on an exercise flying over the Hinlopen Straits when radio contact was lost due to heavy static interference. At the same time the local radar post at Narvik was showing a distorted signal of the jet fighters, as well as the presence of a UFO.

While the jets were circling, the flight leader Captain Olaf Larsen spotted a large metallic disc in the snow, which looked as if it had crashed. He reported his findings and search and recovery teams were sent to the location.

When the teams arrived they found a craft, one-hundred-and-fifty feet in diameter, that was giving off radioactive emissions. The craft was silver in colour and had strange symbols written on the outside. The teams assumed that this was a Russian test aircraft that had flown out of control. It was shipped to Narvik where it was examined.

The results of the investigation were not released for two years. The German newspapers said that the report concluded that the craft was not of Russian origin and that it had not been built by any country on Earth. The material the craft was made from could not be identified.

Flying Saucers Cometh

Although strange phenomena have been seen in the skies around the world for centuries, in 1947 they were inadvertently given a name that captured the popular imagination. The man responsible was a thirty-two-year-old businessman named Kenneth Arnold.

Born in Minnesota in 1915, Arnold attended college on an athletics scholarship, but a knee injury dashed any hope of a career in American football. After he graduated, he set up his own business in Boise, Idaho, designing and marketing fire-fighting equipment. He sold his products across the north-western states and, to visit clients, he learnt to fly, took a pilot's licence and bought a small Callair plane. On 24 June 1947, Arnold clinched a deal in Chehalis, Washington state. His next stop was Yakima, which lay to the east, the other side of the Cascade mountains.

Arnold was also an official air rescue search pilot and he

Kenneth Arnold.

planned to spend some time over the Cascades, searching for a transport aeroplane that had been lost in the area some weeks before. A reward had been offered for finding the wreckage.

It was a clear, sunny day and Arnold spent about an hour searching the area around Mount Rainier. Finding nothing, he turned east for Yakima, flying at an altitude of around 10,000 feet. Suddenly, his plane was lit up by a bright flash. At first, he thought it was the sunlight reflected from a military jet buzzing him, but a visual scan of the sky revealed only a four-engined DC-4 freight plane to port and about fifteen miles behind him. Then he saw a flash in the direction of Mount Baker, 140 miles to the north of Mount Rainier.

Suddenly a formation of nine bright objects came speeding southward towards him. The flashes were sunlight from their metal surfaces, and the whole formation travelled with a strange undulating motion. Eight of the objects were boomerang shaped, but the leading object appeared to be shaped like two boomerangs stuck together.

Arnold turned his plane to get a clearer view. He opened a side window of the cockpit and watched the objects weaving among the peaks of the mountain range. An experienced pilot, Arnold was adept at estimating distance in the air. He estimated that the formation was a hundred miles away when he first saw it and he realised that they must be travelling at an incredible speed. He set about making detailed observations that would help him work out the size and speed of the objects. As the objects passed over a snow-covered ridge, he noted that lead object left the southern end of the ridge as the last one reached the northern end.

As the strange, undulating line of objects passed ahead of his little plane, he timed how long it took for the objects to cover the distance from Mount Rainier to the southern-most crest of Mount Adams, around fifty miles to the south-east. After that, they disappeared. They were travelling at such a speed that the whole sighting had lasted under three minutes.

Arnold was intrigued and excited. Seattle in Washington state was one of the great centres of aircraft design and he was convinced that he had seen the very latest jet aircraft. When he landed at Yakima, he told several people about what he had seen. Then he sat down with a map. Arnold found that the snow-covered ridge the formation had flown over – and hence the formation itself – was five miles long. Then he did some rough calculations based on the timings he had taken and worked out that the objects were travelling at some 1,200 miles an hour, twice the speed of sound, a feat that many still thought was impossible.

Kenneth Arnold with a drawing of the UFO he saw over Mount Rainier.

Later that afternoon, Arnold flew on to Pendleton, Oregon. There, to his surprise, he was greeted by a crowd of people, including a number of newspaper reporters. News of his mysterious sighting had been radioed ahead from Yakima. In Pendleton,

Arnold sat down to check his figures. He obtained a more accurate distance between Mount Rainier and Mount Adams. And when he recalculate the speed of the mysterious objects he discovered that they were travelling at an astonishing 1,700 miles an hour. Even Arnold did not believe this and he cautiously continued to quote his previous figure to the press.

The next day, a man stopped Arnold in the street. He claimed to have seen similar objects just hours before Arnold had made his sighting. This convinced Arnold that he had seen something truly extraordinary. Perhaps it had not been the latest US jet at all, but something more sinister; the Soviets' latest secret weapon, perhaps. And he decided to report the matter to the FBI. He went to the local FBI office, but it was closed. So Arnold went to the offices of the local newspaper office and told the full story to journalists there.

The newspaper ran the story, using Arnold's description of the sighting and quoting his estimate of the objects' speed. It was in that story that the term 'flying saucer' was invented. Arnold did not describe what he had seen as flying saucers. Nor did he say that he had seen something that looked like a saucer. However, he had used the word saucer: describing the objects, he said: 'Their flight was like speedboats on rough water, or similar to the tail of a Chinese kite that I once saw blowing in the wind. Or maybe it would be best to describe their flight characteristics as very similar to a formation of geese, in a rather diagonal chain-like line, as if they were linked together. As I put it to newsmen in Pendleton, Oregon, they flew like a saucer would if you skipped it across the water. They fluttered and sailed, tipping their wings alternately and emitting those very bright blue-white flashes from their surfaces.'

So it was their movement that was like that of a saucer, not the shape of them.

After the paper ran the story, it put it out on the Associated Press newswires. The newswire subtly changed the story. Their bulletin ran: 'Nine bright saucer-like objects flying at "incredible speed" at 10,000 feet altitude were reported here today by Kenneth Arnold, a Boise, Idaho pilot, who said he could not hazard a guess as to what they were.'

Pilot Kenneth Arnold saw UFOs flying by Mount Rainer, Washington State, USA on 24 June 1947.

The story caught the media's imagination. It went around the world and, in the process, the term 'flying saucer' caught on. Arnold found himself besieged by the media. The following day he told the local radio station, KWRC: 'I at first thought they were geese, because [they] flew like geese, but [they were] going so fast that I immediately changed my mind and decided it was a bunch of new jet planes in formation... like I told the Associated Press, I'd be glad to confirm it with my hands on a Bible because I did see it, and whether it has anything to do with our army or our intelligence, or whether it has to do with some foreign country, I don't know. But I did see it and I did clock it, and I just happened to be in a beautiful position to do it, and it's just as much a mystery to me as it is to everyone else who's been calling me the last twenty-four hours, wondering what it was.'

Belatedly, the FBI got on the case. Their report says: '[Arnold]... would have to be strongly convinced that he actually saw something before he would report such an incident and open himself up for the ridicule that would accompany such a report.'

Arnold was also contacted by two US Air Force pilots, Captain E.J. Smith and his co-pilot Ralph Stevens, who claimed to have seen similar craft. The three men met up in Seattle in 1947 and compared notes.

There was yet another independent witness to Arnold's sighting.

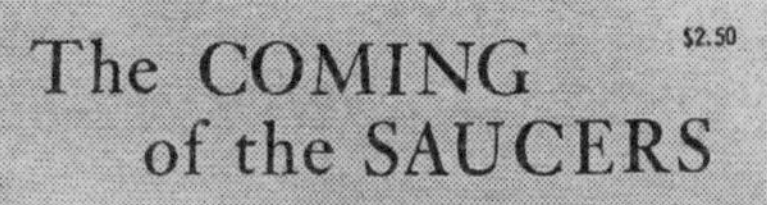

Cover of *The Coming of the Saucers* by Kenneth Arnold and Ray Palmer (1952)

It came from a prospector named Fred Johnson who had seen the objects from the ground. He shied away from going to the newspapers. Instead, he contacted the US Army with his story.

He said that on the afternoon of 24 June, he had been prospecting in the Cascade mountains when a formation of flying objects had passed overhead at around 1,000 feet.

'Their speed as far as I know seemed to be greater than anything I ever saw,' he said.

Altogether he thought that there were five or six objects in the formation. He was carrying a telescope and turned it on one of them. It was oval, he said, with a pointed nose and tail that 'looked like the big hand of a clock and shifted from side to side'. The last he saw of the discs, they were standing on edge, banking away into a cloud. He also noticed that the needle of his compass swung about wildly while they were around. But once they had gone, it settled down.

A month after the sighting, Arnold was flying to Maury Island in Puget Sound, when he saw another chain of objects approaching him at high speed. This time there were twenty-five of them.

'I was a little bit shocked and excited when I realised that they had the same flight characteristics as the large objects I had observed,' he said.

He turned his plane to follow them, but they disappeared at high speed. He was sure that they could not have been birds – they travelled too fast. Later he discovered that local farmers had reported seeing an unusual flight of 'birds' that morning. Having already been in the centre of a media circus, this time Arnold refrained from telling the press or the authorities.

Arnold's interest in UFOs did not end there. He took to investigating other sightings and has been called the world's first UFOlogist. In 1952, he published *The Coming of the Saucers*, co-written by the publisher of *Amazing Stories*, Ray Palmer, who quickly founded *Fate* magazine, the first dedicated UFO publication.

In 1977, Arnold was the guest of honour at a UFO convention called to celebrate the 30th anniversary of this Mount Rainier sighting. Otherwise he kept his distance from enthusiasts. He did not believe that flying saucers were alien spacecraft, rather he thought that they were some kind of living creature that lived high up in the Earth's atmosphere. He died in 1984.

Fate magazine: cover of the first issue in 1948, with Kenneth Arnolds UFO sighting depicted.

The Site of the Sighting

Since Kenneth Arnold's first encounter with flying saucers there in 1947, the Cascades have been a rich source of sightings, particularly in the mid-1960s. Sightings reached another peak in the 1970s when local firemen were alerted to glowing balls of light being observed in the Yakima Indian Reserve, just east of the Cascades. UFOlogist David Ackers was called in to investigate.

'There was one spooky one which just crept up on me,' he said. 'The object had the shape of a large brownish-orange ball which flickered slightly.'

Ackers concluded that there was UFO activity going on, but there was no conclusive proof that it was extraterrestrial in origin. Writer Paul Devereux, who is a leading proponent of the 'earthlight' theory of UFOs, points to the Cascades as a natural home for that phenomenon. According to the earthlight theory, glowing lights in the sky and other anomalies that are interpreted as UFOs are caused by electromagnetic fields generated by the build-up of strains in the Earth's crust. The Cascades are subject to just such geological disturbances. Geological surveys say there was a lull in seismic activity in the area at the time of Arnold's sighting. But Devereux says the geological stresses were building and there was an earthquake in the area in 1949.

However, Arnold was an experienced pilot and was trained in the observational skills required by a search pilot. Few can doubt that he knew what he saw. Despite the scoffing of sceptics, his sighting has stood the test of time and in all the years since he saw the first flying saucer no one has proved him wrong.

Island of Intrigue

After his first sighting over the Cascades, Kenneth Arnold saw another formation of UFOs flying over Maury Island in Washington state. He was not alone. On 23 June 1947, the day before Arnold made his famous 'flying saucer' sighting, Tacoma harbour patrolman Harold A. Dahl, his fifteen-year-old son, another crew member and the Dahl's dog set off by boat to patrol Puget Sound. The day was overcast. The sky was thick with grey clouds and it looked as if it was going to rain. Anticipating a storm, Dahl decided to take shelter in a bay on Maury Island, opposite Tacoma, which was about two miles away across the water. On the way, six doughnut-shaped UFOs appeared overhead. Dahl and crew were stunned. Then, menacingly, one of the objects began to descend.

The UFO was around a hundred feet in diameter and it had a hole in the middle. It appeared to be made of metal. On the outer rim there were two portholes but the inner side of the doughnut was lined with round windows. Dahl quickly beached his vessel, then climbed out and took four photographs of the UFO.

The UFOs seemed to take this amiss. Without warning, one of them sprayed the beach with molten metal. The red-hot shower hit the boat, killing the dog and severely burning the arm of Dahl's son. Then the UFOs rose into the sky and disappeared towards the Pacific.

Dahl reported the encounter to his superior officer, Fred L. Crisman. The following morning, a mysterious black-clad stranger arrived at Dahl's home in a black Buick sedan car and invited him out for breakfast. Dahl was amazed when the man revealed that he knew about the encounter the previous day.

'Silence is the best thing for you and your family,' the man whispered conspiratorially. 'You should not have seen what you have seen.'

Dahl was a good, law-abiding citizen, and the meeting left him shaken and perplexed.

Although Maury Island is just twenty miles away from the Cascade Mountains, it is fairly cut off from the rest of the world and Dahl knew nothing of Kenneth Arnold's fateful encounter that day. However, *Amazing Stories*' publisher Ray Palmer heard of the sighting at Maury Island, and he offered Arnold $200 to investigate the case. $200 was not to be sniffed at in 1947 and Arnold plunged himself into what was to become one of the most contentious cases in the history of UFOlogy.

On 29 July, Arnold flew to Tacoma to start his investigation. He was on his way when he made his second sighting. When he arrived, he headed for the Winthrop Hotel and was surprised to find that a room had already been booked in his name, even though no one was supposed to know that he was in town. But Arnold put this down to a lucky coincidence and set about tracking down Dahl.

After his meeting with the man in black, Dahl was naturally circumspect. He refused to meet Arnold, saying the encounter had brought him nothing but bad luck. He even suggested that Arnold ditch the investigation and head back to Idaho where he belonged. But Arnold was persistent and eventually persuaded Dahl to come to his room at the Winthrop, where Dahl explained what he had seen.

Dahl turned up again the following morning at 9:30 a.m. Arnold was still asleep and he was woken by Dahl banging on the door. This time, Dahl was not alone. He was with Crisman, his command officer, and Crisman was doing all the talking. He said that he had been out to the island to check out Dahl s story. There was debris all over the island, he said.

Arnold naturally wanted to see the debris for himself, but first he decided to enlist some help. He called Captain E.J. Smith, one of the other witnesses to his Mount Rainier sighting, who he had recently met in Seattle, and explained the situation. Smith was eager to help and, on 30 July, Arnold went to pick him up in his plane.

That afternoon, with Smith now ensconced at the Winthrop, Dahl and Crisman returned to the hotel and told Smith their stories. After a thorough cross-examination of the pair, Smith asked Crisman and Dahl to supply samples of the debris. He also wanted to see Dahl s photographs. And he asked them to organise a meeting with Dahl s crewman and a trip to the island.

Later that evening, out of the blue, Arnold got a phone call from Ted Morello, a journalist from the United Press. Morello said that details of private conversations between Arnold and Smith had been leaked to him by an anonymous caller. Arnold suspected Dahl and Crisman, but Morello knew what had been said when Arnold and Smith had been alone in the room. Arnold then suspected that the room was bugged, but an exhaustive search of the room found nothing. Arnold was now beginning to regret that he had got himself involved.

Smith and Arnold s suspicions were further aroused the following day when Crisman, Dahl and his crewman arrived with samples of the debris as requested. Arnold noted that the fragments did not match Dahl's descriptions. They looked and felt no like ordinary aircraft metal. The photographs were not forthcoming either. Arnold attempted to apply pressure by telling Crisman that he was going to involve US Air Force Intelligence. Although this did not faze Crisman at all, Arnold was prepared. As good his word, he phoned Lieutenant Brown, an intelligence officer at Hamilton Field Air Force Base in California who had a history of investigating UFO reports. He agreed to lend his expertise to the investigation.

But even as he was making his call, Arnold saw Smith and Crisman rapt in a private conversation. He then began to believe that it was Smith that was leaking their private conversations. After all, he was an officer in the Air Force.

Later that day, Brown and a colleague called Davidson flew to Tacoma in a B-25. They came to the Winthrop. Crisman duly arrived and related both his own and Dahl's story. Arnold noticed that Brown showed little interest in Crisman's account, as if he had heard it all before. When Crisman had finished, Brown and his colleague immediately made their excuses and set off back to Hamilton Field with the box of the so-called 'debris'.

Events, already suspicious, now turned down right sinister. The following day, Arnold got a call from Crisman telling him that Brown's B-25 had crashed some twenty minutes after taking off from Tacoma. Both Brown and Davidson had been killed, Crisman said. Arnold could not believe his ears, but the report was confirmed by Smith who had verified the news with Brown's superiors.

Arnold then began to fear for his own life. He called Ray Palmer and told him what had happened to Brown and Davidson. He said he was quitting the investigation and heading home. Under the circumstances, Palmer advised Arnold not to take any remaining fragments with him on the plane home.

Before Arnold left, Crisman took him to see the boat that he said had been damaged in the encounter. But when Arnold saw it, it was obvious that it was not the same boat that Dahl had taken to Maury Island on 23 June. And Crisman still failed to produce the photographs. In despair, Arnold returned to the Winthorp. He was packing when got a call from Morello.

The anonymous informant had informed Morello that Brown and Davidson's plane was shot down. On 2 August, the *Tacoma Times* carried the headline: 'Sabotage Hinted in Crash of Army Bomber at Kelso.' The article speculated that the plane had been hit by a 20mm cannon to stop the Maury Island 'flying saucer debris' from reaching Hamilton Field Air Force Base. Morello also hinted that Arnold's aircraft would be shot at.

Arnold was now completely freaked. He and Smith went to find Dahl, who informed them that Crisman had left town. Morello confirmed that Crisman had embarked on an army bomber bound for Alaska. Smith had already received orders return to his post. As the entire investigation fell apart, Arnold was eager to make himself scarce too.

It was now too late to fly home and Arnold decided to stay on in Tacoma overnight. The following morning, he decided to say goodbye to Dahl before leaving. But when he arrived at Dahl's home he found the house derelict. And there was no sign of Dahl.

By then only thing that concerned Arnold was getting home in one piece. He took off from Tacoma in trepidation. Everything went smoothly until he made a refuelling stop in Pendleton, Oregon. After that, on the final leg of the journey to Idaho, his engine cut out. He was sure that he was going the same way as Brown and Davidson. But he was in small plane that could glide, and he had the skill to land the plane in one piece.

With Arnold out of the way, the investigation was taken over by an Army Intelligence officer from McChord Field. The case, he said, was a hoax and the associated deaths and disappearances mere coincidences. However, for those who understood the machinations of government, this pat explanation suggested a cover-up. Plainly, someone had gone to great lengths to sandbag the Maury Island investigation. They were willing to kill to prevent the truth coming out. But who were they, and why were they doing this?

Four years later UFOlogist John Keel claimed to have the answer. He reckons that Crisman had been in cahoots with Ray

Palmer for years and, after Arnold's sighting in the Cascades had made headlines, they had dreamt up the Maury Island mystery. Crisman had recruited Dahl into the conspiracy, then tried to persuade Palmer to run the story in *Amazing Stories.* Lieutenant Brown showed no interest in Crisman's story because it was so plainly a hoax. According to Keel, Brown did not even take the debris on the plane with him back to Hamilton Field Air Force Base and the crash was merely a coincidence.

Strangely, although Keel is convinced that Crisman and Dahl's story was an invention, he believes that something strange did occur on Maury Island on 23 June 1947. Dahl's son's injuries and the death of the dog bear this out. The key, Keel maintains, lies in the strange molten metal deposited on the boat. Keel believes that this came from the Atomic Energy Commission plutonium processing plant in nearby Hanford, Washington. The Maury Island encounter, he reckons, was simply a case of the illegal dumping of radioactive waste dropped by plane in the sound.

Then we come to Dahl's mysterious black-clad visitor. According to Keel, he was simply a security agent of the AEC, who had traced Dahl from the records of his son who was then in hospital with radiation burns. The AEC hardly wanted evidence of illegal dumping of nuclear waste being published far and wide. That's why he had warned Dahl to keep quiet.

You may find Keel's argument is convincing. It may be the truth. But we will never know what really happened at Maury Island that night. Crisman and Dahl, the men who hold all the answers, have not resurfaced since their disappearance in 1947, so we will have to make do with the official findings.

On 27 April 1949, a report on UFO sightings entitled 'Project Saucer' was issued by the Air Materials Command at Wright Field, Dayton, Ohio. As part of its investigation, it published details of the analysis of the Maury Island debris. Its findings were that the crude material sample was magnetic and the debris contained minerals such as iron oxide; about 21 per cent of the sample was soluble in hydrochloric acid. The part of the residue that was insoluble was non-magnetic. Since there were obviously two different chemical components, they were tested separately. The acid-soluble fraction was 49.7 per cent iron with traces of the heavy metals molybdenum and cadmium. No copper, nickel or cobalt was found. The remainder of this faction was largely oxygen. The fraction that was acid insoluble contained manganese and manganese oxide, iron and iron oxide, calcium and calcium oxide, and barium and barium oxide. The report's conclusion was that all these substances were terrestrial in origin, implying that the Maury Island encounter was a hoax. However, the debris samples have never been submitted to independent analysis.

History as we Know it?

Antique Astronauts

In the thirty years following World War II, humankind made its technological leap into space. At the same time flying saucers began buzzing the earth in ever increasing numbers and reports of alien encounters became commonplace.

But some people began to wonder if aliens had only just started visiting the Earth. We now saw their craft as spaceship and the aliens themselves as astronauts only because we had recently become familiar with these ideas. If they had been visiting us in ancient times, say, they would have been seen completely differently.

An early advocate of the idea was Desmond Leslie, who co-authored the best-selling *Flying Saucers Have Landed* with UFO contactee George Adamski in 1953. Leslie began looking for evidence that space visitors had come to Earth before. He turned to ancient literature. In the Vedic literature of India, written between 1,500 and 500 BCE, he found references to *vimanas* or 'airboats'. Leslie realised that the flying saucers seen in the 1940s and 1950s were only an interplanetary, more advanced, model of the ancient *vimana*. He also looked into Celtic myth and found ancient heroes such as Chuchulain of Ireland, who had at their disposal weapons that bore a striking resemblance to modern-day missiles and tanks. And hieroglyphics on the ceiling of the Temple of Abydos in

Atlantis depicted on cover of *FATE* magazine, July 1953.

Egypt, built over five thousand years ago, clearly shows modern military technology, including gunboats, a helicopter, a submarine, a plane and a gun.

Leslie deduced that a race of space people had come to Earth before the Flood and interbred with Earthlings. Their hybrid offspring founded what we now known as the civilisation of Atlantis. And he is not alone in this belief. Many people believe that alien intervention explains the great leap humankind made when our ape-like ancestors came down from the trees and suddenly spawned vast, complex civilisations.

It has also been suggested that ancient monuments, such as the pyramids, were built by ancient astronauts. Some five thousand years ago, it is said, a giant UFO swooped down over the desert at Gisa. Its energy beams cut and moved huge stone blocks into place while astonished desert nomads looked on. The craft then flew off leaving behind them three huge pyramids. The amazed onlookers would have had no words to describe what they saw. For generations, they would recount in their legends and their sacred texts that they had received a visit from god. After all, the ancient Egyptian god, Re, rides across the sky in a fiery chariot.

Egyptian pyramids.

According to this theory, the ancient astronauts also intervened to build other, otherwise unexplainable ancient monuments – Stonehenge in England, the giant statues on Easter Island and the curious pyramids of Latin America. No one knows why these advanced alien civilisations

Stonehenge, Wiltshire.

would help the primitive indigenous people to build these huge structures. However, even the sceptics admit that these monuments have an astronomical significance. Perhaps they are gateways to the stars.

Alien Influence

Others believe that the alien visitors made no direct intervention in human history – just as they refrain from direct intervention now. But the mere presence of the aliens and their artefacts gave evolution a nudge – the most famous depiction of this is the opening scenes of Arthur C. Clarke's novel and the movie *2001: A Space Odyssey*.

Mme Blavatsky, the Russian-born founder of the Theosophical Society.

None of these ideas are particularly new. The concept of advanced civilisations from the stars influencing human progress has been around since at least Victorian times, when members of the Theosophical Society, an occult group, imagined an alternative history for the human race. In 1888, the Theosophists' leader Madame Blavatsky published *The Secret Doctrine*, all 1,500 pages of it. It purports to have been based on the world's first book *The Stanzas of Dzyan* which, unfortunately, scholars down the ages have failed to unearth. The heavens, Madame Blavatsky said, are full of numerous universes, each containing countless solar systems. Each solar system had its own god. Beneath him are seven planetary spirits, each in charge of a phalanx of angels. They had all the characteristics of modern-day astronauts.

Evolution, she said, takes place by steps from mineral to vegetable to animal to human to the superhuman or spiritual being who could travel out into space. The first inhabitants of Earth descend-

Atlantis: The Atlantean High Priest Ya-Uli. life XXVII from Annie Besant and C.W. Leadbeater's *The Lives of Alcyone*, 1925.

ed from the residents of the moon and lived on a continent called the 'Imperishable Sacred Land'. Then came the Hyperborean race, also known as the Boneless or the Sweatborn. They lived at the North Pole. But as they did not have bodies, presumably, they did not feel the cold. Next came the Lemurians, who were the first to have bodies and reproduced by sexual intercourse. Their homeland is now at the bottom of the Indian Ocean – Atlantis again.

The fifth of these so-called 'root races' were the Aryans who spread south and west from Northern Asia. Apparently, we are still in the Aryan phase. Madam Blavatsky revealed that there will be two more root races. Then the cycle will be complete and humans will move on to another planet to start all over again. Meanwhile, individual humans progress from having physical bodies, through astral, mental and ethereal, in a series of incarnations. Progress is regulated by your karma. Obviously, those with the best karma have arrived at the highest ethereal state. These are the Masters, superbeings who visited Earth to vouchsafe wisdom to Madame Blavatsky.

Chariots of the Gods

These concepts made global headlines again the 1970s with the work of the Swiss author, Erich von Däniken. In 1968, he wrote *Chariots of the Gods*, which presented evidence for alien visitations in ancient times. After a slow start, it became a world-wide best-seller. Von Däniken followed up with further titles, which unravel all the ancient mysteries in terms of visits from ancient spacemen.

Central to von Däniken's concept is the remarkable consistency of the images and icons of ancient peoples – even though they were spread far and wide across the world. There is also a uniformity to their legends and the characteristics of their gods which could not be put down to chance. He picked up these ideas from his childhood reading of the Bible.

'I was intrigued by the references in the Old Testament which seemed to suggest God travelled by various means of sophisticated transport,' he says. 'After a lot of research, I found that many other ancient peoples recorded similar stories about god-like beings. I decided that the gods must therefore be extraterrestrials.'

There is a similarity in the creation myths and the accounts of visitations from the gods from sources as diverse as the ancient Egyptians, the Maya and the ancient Chinese, who would have had no contact with each other. Von Däniken dismisses the idea that the accounts of flying gods might only be symbolic.

'That's impossible,' he says. 'These "heavenly beings" gave mankind a lot of advanced knowledge – astronomy, for instance – at the dawn of civilisation. This is not symbolism, but fact.'

This memory of visitation by ancient astronauts exists not just in myth and sacred texts. The Kayapo Indians of Brazil – a tribe that has been in existence for over four thousand years – has a ceremony in which a figure appears in a bulky 'space suit' made from basketwork. The figure represents the 'teacher from heaven' and the ceremony commemorates the alien's visit to the tribe.

Von Däniken also turned to ancient Indian texts, in this case the *Mahabharata*, which was written slightly later than the Vedic texts, but borrows much from them. And, like Desmond Leslie before him, von Däniken draws attention to the detailed descriptions of the *virmanas* – a word meaning 'flying machines'. In the text, the *virmanas* are often piloted by Indian gods and are sometimes used for military purposes. In one particularly striking passage, one of them unleashes an *agneya* weapon: 'A blazing missile possessed of the radiance of smokeless fire was discharged. A thick gloom suddenly encompassed the hosts. All points of the compass were suddenly enveloped in darkness. Evil bearing winds began to blow. Clouds reared into the higher air, showering blood. The very elements seemed confused. The sun appeared to spin round. The world, scorched by the heat of that weapon, seemed to be in fever.'

It is not hard to see that this is the description of a nuclear warhead exploding. There is no reason to believe that the ancient Indian civilisation – or indeed any ancient civilisation – had nuclear weapons, so it is easy to conclude that the *virmanas* were of extraterrestrial origin.

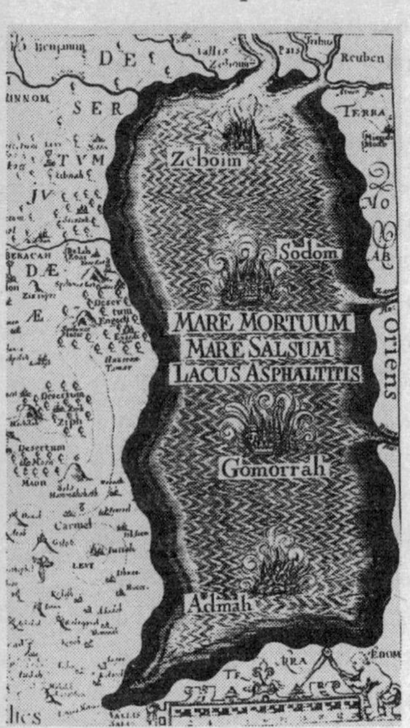

Sodom and Gomorrah in relation to the Dead Sea (*Mare Mortuum*). Engraving from Thomas Fullers *Pisgah-sight of Palestine and the Confines Thereof...* 1650.

It is clear that the story of the destruction of Sodom and Gomorrah in the Bible was also caused by a nuclear blast. First two angels appeared to Lot, the only righteous man in Sodom. They told him to take his family and leave as the two cities were to be destroyed. As they were fleeing, 'the Lord rained upon Sodom and Gomorrah brimstone and fire'. Lot's wife stopped and looked back. She was turned into a pillar of salt. Von Däniken says that the two angels who appeared to Lot were clearly ancient alien astronauts.

According to the Bible, the Red Sea was parted to let the Children of Israel escape from Egypt and the Moses was led to the Promised Land by a pillar of light. These have been interpreted as more examples of alien intervention in human history.

Once ancient history is seen through these eyes, evidence of ancient astronauts is everywhere. Primitive man was obsessed with space-suited figures. Drawings of what look like astronauts are found in cave dwellings in the Americas, Europe, Africa, the Far East and Australia. A figure carved on the rocks of Val Camonica, Italy, is wearing headgear with some kind of aerial sprouting from it. Another helmeted figure appears in a rock carving at Capo di Ponte. Similar figures have been found carved into the ancient petroglyphs of the Toro Muerte desert in Peru. A weird rock art figure at Tassili in the Sahara was nicknamed 'the Martian' by archaeologists. Von Däniken says that it is plainly wearing a spacesuit. An ancient Australian Aboriginal cave drawing made some five thousand years ago shows the same thing.

A space-suited figure in a cave painting on the Russo-Chinese border, painted around 2000 BCE, is holding a disc-shaped communication device. The figure's helmet has two antennae on it and above it there is a flying saucer, emitting a plume of smoke.

Von Däniken also points out that the astonishing cementless masonry of Inca architecture, as well as the erection of the massive stone blocks found in megalithic monuments worldwide, could easily be achieved by alien anti-gravity technology or something similar. He has found Egyptian effigies that bear an astonishing resemblance to modern aircraft and an Aztec incense burner that is shaped like a jet engine. The handle of an Aztec ceremonial knife shows a flying god, and a pre-historic Colombian figurine shows a god wearing a space helmet, as does a Japanese Dogu sculpture, which is over five thousand years old. This figure is also wearing goggles – not a common item in Stone Age Japan.

A carving on the lid of a tomb in the ancient Mayan Temple at Palenque, Mexico, shows a seated figure, wearing a helmet, squeezed into small capsule, crammed with levers and other controls. This is plainly a space ship, though experts in Maya mythology insist that it shows the symbolic descent of a dead man's soul into the underworld.

A small sculpture showing a figure in a space capsule was unearthed at Toprakkale in Turkey. Although some have tried to dismiss it as a hoax, it is three thousand years old. The four-thousand-year-old Lolladoff plate from Nepal clearly shows a disc-shaped UFO and the figure of a classic 'Grey', as seen by modern abductees. Other flying saucers appear in a Neolithic cave painting in south-west France, painted five thousand years ago. It shows wildlife in a landscape, with disc-shaped UFOs hovering above.

Curiously, a humanoid figure near one of the UFOs has a tail.

But more disturbing is the evidence of a deformed skull on show at the Museum of the Inca in Peru. It is three thousand years old, and its weird elongated head-shape is also seen in ancient Egyptian reliefs. Von Däniken maintains that the head was deliberately stretched to ape the head-shape of alien visitors. Others say that it is the product of some early genetic experiment.

The Ark of the Covenant.

The lost Ark of the Covenant, the gold-plated chest in which Moses put the tablets of stone containing the Ten Commandments, may hold another clue. No ordinary person can touch it, otherwise they would die. Von Däniken says that it was essentially a condenser and anyone who touched it would be electrocuted. The two gold cherubs on the top were antennae – the whole thing was a radio set, which allowed, Moses to communicate with the 'Lord' in the mothership above. But in *The Sign and the Seal,* journalist Graham Hancock maintains that it was a nuclear weapon and anyone who touched it would die from radiation sickness.

Von Däniken has also found one of the alien's landing sites. These are the so-called Nazca lines, a vast array of ancient lines and drawings on the Plain of Nazca in the Peruvian Andes, which can be seen only from the air. Because there is no rain and little wind on the Nazca plain, these lines have survived since prehistoric times, but they were identified only when people began flying over them in aircraft in the 1930s.

Orthodox archaeologists insist that the Nazca markings are ancient roads. The problem is that they lead nowhere, though there is now a theory that the cities some of the straight lines joined were subsequently destroyed. Others have said that the markings are

Nazca lines on the desert of Peru.

some kind of ancient calendar. But in *Von Däniken's Proof* (1977), he points out, correctly, that the lines show no astronomical alignments. Along with the straight lines, there are markings that look like the parking bays for aircraft at a modern-day airport. Is this where ancient astronauts parked their spaceships? There are patterns – triangles, spirals, a bird, a monkey, a spider and flowers – all hundreds of feet long. They can be seen only from the sky.

Saintbury lay, Gloucestershire runs for about 3½ miles NNW-SSE in the Cotswolds. In this aerial view of the ley, looking south, significant features are circled.

Researchers in Britain and France say that ley lines – the lines that connect ancient monuments that are, again, clearly visible only from above – also hold a clue. Plotted on a map, UFO sightings fall into straight lines that correspond to ancient leys.

The biggest problem with the concept of alien visitation, ancient or modern, is the question of how aliens could travel vast interstellar distances to get here. As far as we can tell, there is no other inhabited planet in our solar system. So the nearest home for another civilisation most be at least 4.2 light years away – on a planet orbiting the nearest star to our sun. Even if a civilisation discovered a way of travelling at close to the speed of light – the theoretical limit – it would take them over eight years to make a round trip, so they would hardly be dropping by for a casual visit. Physicists are now grappling with ways to break this upper limit, possibly by travelling through worm-holes in space and time which join two very distance places. Another theory is that they travel through space relatively slowly on huge, self-sustaining motherships and those craft we see visiting Earth are smaller scout craft. In this scenario, the extraterrestrial race visited our forebears on Earth thousands of years ago and left their indelible mark on human history. Now they are coming back again.

The Offspring of Sirius

Another version of the ancient astronaut idea was outlined by Robert Temple in 1976 in his book The Sirius Mystery. In the book, Temple expands on the findings of two French anthropologists who studied the Dogon people of Mali. According to tribal folklore, the Dogon trace their origins to the Nommo, a race of amphibious creatures who come from a planet orbiting the star Sirius and landed in ships in Egypt five to six thousand years ago. Indeed Sirius was central to ancient Egyptian cosmology. The brightest star in the sky, its first dawn rising each year coincided with the annual flood of the Nile, which was crucial to the agriculture that sustained Egyptian civilisation.

Every half century, the Dogon perform a unique ceremony called the Sigui. In it they celebrate Sirius's twin, a small, heavy star that orbits Sirius once every fifty years. Indeed the star Sirius does have a twin, Sirius B, but it is invisible to the naked eye. Neither the Dogon nor any ancient civilisations possessed the optics necessary to see it. The Dogon also knew that Sirius's companion was super dense, a fact only known to modern science in 1926, just five years before Western anthropologists first contacted the Dogon.

But that is not the limit of their knowledge of the Sirius system.

Dogon priests have known details of the precise orbital period of Sirius B for many centuries. They also know of a third body in the system that has not yet been identified by modern astronomers. The knowledge has been handed down by a secret oral tradition, started long before Western astronomers even knew that Sirius B existed. Plainly, the Dogon could have got their information only from some extraterrestrial source. There is no other explanation.

The Dogon of Mali are an isolated tribe living in a remote area of West Africa. These days there are barely two hundred thousand of them. They live in villages clinging to the steep Bandiagara cliffs east of the Upper Niger River. While they cannot be described as 'primitive' – they have a sophisticated cultural life – they are not technically advanced.

In the late 1940s, two leading French anthropologists, Marcel Griaule and Germaine Dieterlen, spent a long period living with the Dogon. The two scientists eventually won the confidence of the priests, who divulged the secrets of their religious beliefs.

The Dogon's creation myth is tied up with a small star called Po Tolo, which means 'seed star'. The star is also named after the tiniest seed known to them, which they call 'fonio', and is know botanically as *Digitaria exilis*. The smallest seed, for the Dogon, means the beginning of all things. The Dogon believe that creation began with this collapsed star, which is companion of the brilliant Sirius A, or Dog Star. Known astronomically as Sirius B, it is a 'white dwarf' and is visible only through a powerful telescope. It gives off little light and is overwhelmed by Sirius A, which is ten thousand times brighter. Indeed, although Sirius A is 23 times more luminous than our own sun – there are many stars that are far brighter – it is only 8.6 light years from Earth, making it the brightest star in the night sky.

The Dogon possess a startling wealth of astronomical detail about the Sirius system. They know that Po Tolo is massively dense – its weight is out of all proportion to its small size. This is a property of white dwarves, whose density is a million times that of water. Sirius B is 27,000 times denser than our sun. However, astrophysicists discovered this property only in the twentieth century. The Dogon believe that this is due to the presence of sagala, an extremely dense and strong metallic element unknown on earth. Indeed, matter compressed to that extent is metallic. The Dogon also show that the orbit of Sirius B around Sirius A forms an ellipse, with Sirius A at one focus. This idea only arrived in Western astronomy in the early seventeenth century, when Johannes Kepler overturned the idea that heavenly bodies moved in perfect circular paths.

The Dogon believe Sirius B takes fifty years to orbit Sirius A. Modern astronomy has put the actual orbital period at 50.04 years – close enough. The Dogon also say that Sirius B rotates on its own axis, with a period of one earth-year. Modern astronomy does not have equipment powerful enough to check this. Nor can modern astronomers confirm the Dogon claim that there is a third body in the Sirius system. They call this third object Emme Ya, or 'sorghum woman' (sorghum is the local grain). This is either a small star with a single planet orbiting it, or a planet with a large satellite – like the Earth and the Moon. This is said to be the home of their ancestors, the Nommo.

Griaule and Dieterlen published the Dogon's story for the first time in the book, *A Sudanese Sirius System*, in 1950. This piqued the interest of Robert Temple, a Fellow of the Royal Astronomical Society, who then set about investigating their extraordinary claims. As the Dogon have known this information for thousands of year, Temple argues that it must have been come from ancient astronauts.

This idea was not received with universal approval. Indeed, it was greeted with downright hostility by the late Carl Sagan, popular science writer, Ian Ridpath and others. They argued that people from Europe had been exploring Africa for the previous 150 years. Someone could have come across the Dogon during that time, given them the information about the Sirius system, and the Dogon incorporated it into their cosmology. However, the idea that Sirius might have a tiny companion was raised by F.W. Bessel only in Köningsberg, Prussia, in 1844. It was not until 1862, when Alva n Clark made a 45-centimetre lens for the Dearborn Observatory in

Evansville, Indiana, that it was first seen and it was only photographed for the first time in 1970. The idea that there were such things as super-dense stars only came into currency in 1926. Even so, it was hardly the topic of casual conversation. Dieterlen has since shown that one Dogon model of the Sirius system is nearly five hundred years old. And there is plenty of evidence to show that the Dogon's astronomical knowledge is much older than that. According to conventional history, the Dogon are descendants of Greeks who colonised the part of northern Africa that forms modern Libya. The Roman historian Herodotus called them 'Garamantians', after Garamas, the son of the Greek earth goddess Gaia. Like their Greek forebears, the Dogon are preoccupied with numbers. During their time in Libya, they would certainly have been in an excellent position to pick up astronomical knowledge from the neighbouring Egyptians.

With the destruction of Carthage in 146 BCE, they began to move south. Centuries of slow migration brought the Dogon to the Upper Niger River where they settled and interbred with black Africans living there. According to the twentieth-century historian Robert Graves, the last remnants of this wandering tribe now live in a village called Koromantse, about fifty miles from Bandiagara.

During their travels, it seems improbable that the Dogon had access to astronomical instruments, or met people who had a sophisticated knowledge of the workings of the heavens. So it seems likely that whatever astronomical knowledge they have came from the Egypt, at least nine hundred years before.

The Dogon themselves say that their remarkable knowledge of the complex astronomy of the Sirius system came from their distant ancestors, amphibian extraterrestrials, who they call 'Nommos' and who came from the vicinity of Po Tolo, or Sirius B.

The Dogon are very precise about this. They say the Nommos first arrived from the Sirius system in a vessel that spun, or whirled, during its descent, and made a loud noise like the roaring wind. They also recalled that the flying machine skipped as it landed – like a flat stone skimming across water. It churned up the surface of the ground with what the Dogon call 'spurts of blood'. Those who know the Dogon language say that this phrase could equally translate as 'rocket exhaust' and they could be describing the reverse thrust used to land modern spacecraft. At the same time, the Dogon say that a new heavenly body hovered in the sky at some distance. This could have been a 'mother ship' that remained in orbit while a smaller craft was sent down to the surface of the Earth – in the same way as, during the moon landings, the Apollo space capsule stayed in orbit while the lunar module landed on the Moon's surface.

The Dogon say that the Nommos are amphibians – Nommos in the Dogon language means 'associated with water' or 'finding drinking water is essential'. The Dogon say that they normally lived in water, indeed, they were 'masters of the water'. In Dogon art, they are shown as half reptile, half human.

And the Nommos are not entirely unknown elsewhere on Earth. Representations of the Nommos in Dogon ceremonial carvings bear a striking resemblance to the Babylonian fish-tailed 'demi-god' Oannes, the Akkadians' Nommos-like amphibians known as Ea, the Sumerian Enki and the depiction in some early Egyptian religious art of the goddess Isis in mermaid form. All these figures were supposed to be the progenitors of their particular civilisations.

While the Dogon's knowledge is preserved as a living tradition, much of the knowledge of the Babylonians, Akkadians and ancient Egyptians have been lost. However, it is known that Isis was associated with Sirius, and her consort Osiris was linked to the Dog Star's dark companion. In the temple to Isis at Denderah, the Chapel of the New Year is constructed so that the light from Sirius is channelled down a shaft into the chamber within. This is reminiscent of the Dogon's Sigui ceremony, which is held in the village of Yougo Dogorou when Sirius is visible through a cleft of a rock. Osiris was also the god of the afterlife and Egyptians believed that their immortal souls would live in the heavens with him.

The UFOlogists

Stanton Friedman

Nuclear physicist Stanton Friedman is one of America's leading UFOlogists and has been researching the subject for over forty years, ever since a one-dollar book he bought in 1959 sparked his interest. He co-wrote *Crash at Corona* – the definitive study of the Roswell incident –with Don Berliner. In *TOP SECRET/MAJIC*, he investigated the Majestic-12 documents and US government efforts to conceal evidence of alien spacecraft from the American people. He has lectured around the world. He says that he silenced all but a handful of sceptics who refuse to believe that the Earth is being visited by intelligently controlled extraterrestrial spacecraft.

Curiously, Friedman has never seen a flying saucer himself. Instead he is a critical judge of other people's reports. Nevertheless, he says that seeing UFOs is much more common than most people imagine. At his lectures, he asks people whether they have seen a flying saucer. The hands go up reluctantly, he says, 'but they know I'm not going to laugh'. Typically, ten per cent of the audience admit to seeing a UFO. Then he asks how many of them reported it.

'I'm lucky if it's ten per cent of the ten per cent,' says Friedman. 'Sightings of flying saucers are common, reports are not.'

Friedman became interested in the world of UFOs by accident when he was twenty-four. He was ordering books by mail and needed to buy one more to avoid paying shipping charges. The one he chose was *The Report On Unidentified Flying Objects* by Air Force Captain Edward Ruppelt, former director of Project Blue Book. Friedman read the book and was intrigued. He figured that Ruppelt had to know what he was talking about. So he read fifteen more books on UFOs and spent a couple of years digging up as much information as he could.

His conclusion was that there was overwhelming evidence that Earth is being visited by intelligently controlled extraterrestrial spacecraft. However, he believed that, while some flying saucers are alien space ships, most are not. He believes that, since July 1947 when two crashed saucers were recovered in New Mexico along with alien bodies, the government has back-engineered spacecraft of its own. Only a few insiders know that this has been done and he calls the cover-up the 'Cosmic Watergate'.

He began investigating the Roswell incident in 1978 after being put in touch with one of the witnesses. He has now interviewed over two hundred witnesses – of those some thirty were involved with the discovery and recovery of the alien craft, and the subsequent cover-up of the two crashes. On top of that he has news cuttings from Chicago to the West Coast newspapers on 8 July 1947 and FBI memos that back the story. He also believes that these show that there was a second UFO crash in New Mexico in 1947, 150 miles to the west of Corona, the first crash site, in the plains around San Augustin. He has found eyewitnesses who saw a 'a large metallic object' stuck in the ground there.

He is not convinced by Ray Santilli's alien autospy film though, seeing nothing in it that was associated with a crashed saucer at Roswell or anywhere else. He is also concerned that Santilli has refused to have the film verified. Nor has he released details of the cameraman so that they can be checked out. Friedman likes to look at the evidence.

Friedman is not flattered by being called a UFOlogist. He says that it is supposed to mean a person who has studied the science of UFOlogy, but there are no standards.

'Anybody who reads two books and carries a briefcase thinks he qualifies,' he says.

A big part of the problem of proving that flying saucers really exist is that people make wild claims that cannot be substantiated by the evidence. But he is more annoyed at the failure of the media to do their job. They have failed to dig into what Friedman considers to be the biggest story of the millennium. He believes that the media pay too much attention to what he calls the 'noisy negativists', none of whose arguments stand up under careful scrutiny, he says. 'They sound good, until you look at the evidence and they collapse of their own weight.'

He points out that there have been five large-scale scientific studies on UFOs, ten doctoral theses have been published and hundreds of papers have been produced by scientists. But most people, especially the debunkers, seem to be totally ignorant of this enormous amount of information. In his lectures he goes through the five scientific studies and asks how many people have read them. Less than two per cent of these people, who are plainly interested in the topic, are familiar with even one of the studies.

Friedman is also invited to speak to government bodies and gets a good response. But he finds that the question-and-answer sessions with government people are a one-way street. They ask him a lot of questions but they do not reveal anything. He has spoken at Los Alamos National Laboratory and pulled a huge crowd. He has also given testimony to Congressional hearings in 1968 and at the United Nations in 1978.

Friedman finds that being trained as a scientist is very useful in his work as a UFOlogist. It has meant that his approach is objective, painstaking, honest and scientific. Much of what he worked on as a scientist was classified. He wrote classified documents and had a security clearance. This gave him the opportunity to find out how security works and was good training for searching government archives for classified material later. Now he now lives in Canada and works on less sensitive science research projects such as pollution control and food irradiation.

He believes that the Majestic-12 documents prove President Harry Truman set up a super-secret group of top people from the fields of science, the military and intelligence to learn about alien spacecraft. He has spent over twelve years trawling through fifteen government archives, checking out whether these documents are real. Repeatedly, he has found confirmation of details in the documents that no one but insiders could have known. Friedman has even collected $1,000 from one critic who claimed one of the typefaces used in one of the MJ-12 documents was wrong.

'It was an absurd challenge, since I'd spent weeks searching through the government archives and he hadn't,' says Friedman. 'It also typifies the intellectual bankruptcy of the pseudo-science of anti-UFOlogy. I've yet to see a good anti MJ-12 argument.'

Friedman has had no chance to check out the data on alien abductions, but believes that every abduction story should be taken on its own merits. He has faith in abduction researchers because of his dealings with them and thinks that some people have been abducted.

According to Friedman's theory the government used five major arguments for withholding evidence from the public. The first is that it wants to figure out how flying saucers work because they make wonderful weapons delivery and defence systems. Secondly, it needs to do this before any potential enemy does. Thirdly, if this information was released, the younger generation would see humankind merely as 'earthlings' – which is what we are from an alien point of view. Friedman thinks this would be a great benefit. The problem with that is that there is no government on earth that wants its citizens to owe their primary allegiance to the planet rather than their country. Fourthly, there certain religious fundamentalists who maintain humankind is the only intelligent life in the universe – that means UFOs must be the work of the devil. These fundamentalists have huge political influence and their religions would be destroyed if they were proved wrong. Fifth, any announcement that the aliens were here would cause panic. Some people would believe that aliens are here to slaughter us. Others would reason that the aliens were obviously more technologically advanced than us and would bring with them new energy sources, new transportation systems, new computers and new communication systems. So the stock market would crash and there would be untold economic consequences.

However, Friedman still believes that the public is ready to hear the truth about UFOs. There would, of course, be some people who did not want to know – just as there are five per cent of the

American public who do not believe that man has been to the moon. But the evidence about UFOs could be presented honestly and openly.

'I certainly don't think we should put technical data about flying saucers out on the table,' he says. 'But our planet is being visited by intelligent aliens. It's time we grew up.'

Jaques Vallee

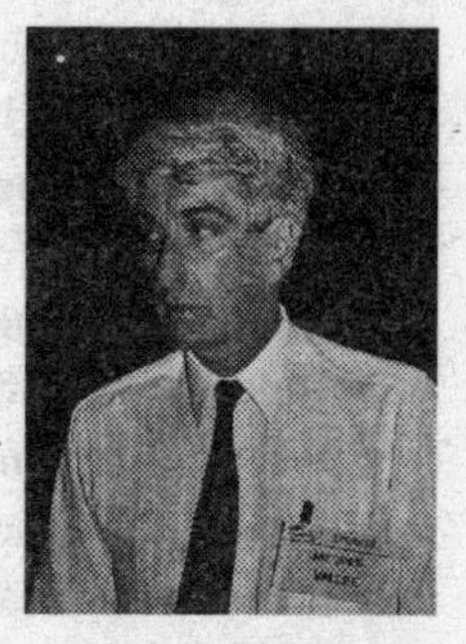

Steven Spielberg's movie *Close Encounters of the Third Kind* made Jacques Vallee the most famous UFOlogist in the world. The François Truffaut character is based on the French researcher. Although he became a computer scientist for the Department of Defense, Vallee began his career as an astrophysicist. As a young man, it was curiosity that led him to study astronomy, but that same curiosity led him on into the world of UFOs. He does not find studying anomalous phenomena unscientific, pointing out that Nobel prize winner Niels Bohr said that all science starts with an anomaly.

He was working at the Paris Observatory when he first got interest in UFOs. They had observed a number of 'unidentified satellites'. However, when the scientists there were ordered destroy the data concerning these 'anomalies' instead of sending it to their colleagues for further study, he rebelled.

This was during the early 1960s when the idea that UFOs were connected to alien intervention was widespread. Back then, he found that the 'extraterrestrial hypothesis' seemed to match witnesses' accounts. But since then, thousands more cases have been-reported and statistical models could be used to analyse them. This has forced Vallee to take another, more critical look at the extraterrestrial hypothesis.

Vallee already had a passion for religious history, myths, occultism and parapsychology and, around 1968, he realised that many aspects of the UFO phenomenon were also present in the folklore of every culture. By 1975, he got the idea of combining these disciplines by considering the UFO phenomenon, not as simply a manifestation of extraterrestrial visitors, but as a control system that had been in existence since the beginning of humankind. He points out that UFO sightings did not start with Kenneth Arnold in 1947. Elements of the phenomena existed before. He believes that the wheels of Ezekiel, cherubim and burning bushes seen in Biblical times, the flying goblins in luminous chariots of the Middle Ages, the phantom airships of the nineteenth century, the 'ghost rockets' of 1946 and the extraterrestrial spacecraft seen today are all essentially the same phenomenon.

As we learn more about the history and geographical distribution of the phenomenon, the standard extraterrestrial hypothesis leads to glaring contradictions, Vallee says. He believes that objects and beings connected to the UFO phenomenon are symbolic, or even theatrical, manifestations, rather than a systematic alien exploration where abductions are conducted for the purposes of so-called 'biological studies', as other UFOlogists suggest.

'We are also looking at some form of non-human consciousness,' he says. 'However, one must be wary of concluding that we are dealing with an "extraterrestrial race".'

Vallee aims to shatter the assumption that 'UFO' means 'extraterrestrial spacecraft'. He believes that behind these enigmatic luminous phenomena is a form of intelligence capable of manipulating space-time and influencing human evolution. In his best-selling book *Confrontations*, published in 1990, he analysed over a hundred UFO encounters using scientific methods, and concludes that the aliens visiting us come from another dimension.

Vallee is the champion of a bold new speculative physics. He believes that objects capable of gradually appearing and disappearing on the spot are modifying space-time topology. This validates the multidimensional models of the universe that theoretical physicists have been working on in recent years.

But he does not totally reject the extraterrestrial hypothesis, just the hard-nosed American approach to it. He believes that we share our existence with other forms of consciousness that influence the topology of our environment and affect the human mind psychically. Vallee has been accused of contradicting himself, because at times he emphasises the physical and material aspects of UFOs, while at others stressing the psychic and paranormal side. But this contradiction is in the data, he says.

Vallee is a believer in alien abduction, but believes that hypnotising abductees as practised in America is unethical, unscientific and perhaps even dangerous. He had investigated over seventy abduction cases. From his interviews with witnesses he has no doubt that the large majority of abductees have had a close encounter with an object emitting electromagnetic radiation, pulsed at hyper-frequencies. The effects on the human brain of these are unknown, so hypnotising the victims could put them at risk. He points out that UFO encounters are dangerous enough to humans as it is, with large amounts of energy confined to a restricted space.

One of the abduction cases Vallee studied was that of Franck Fontaine, who was abducted on 26 November 1979 from the Parisian suburb of Cergy-Pontoise after seeing a bright light in the sky. Vallee was particularly interested in the case because he was born in Pontoise and went to the same school as Fontaine. Although Fontaine admitted, two years later, that the abduction was a hoax, Vallee does not believe the explanations that have been given. They do not correspond to his knowledge of the area or the psychological state of the witnesses.

'I don't believe it was a UFO, but I do think that Franck was actually abducted,' he says. 'Someone is hiding something.'

The dozen or so 'implants' he has examined have not been mysterious in nature. Analysis showed that many of them were the tips of rusty needles, fragments of insects or other natural material embedded in the flesh. However, Vallee was the first to draw attention to the subject of animal mutilations over twenty years ago in his book *La Grande Manipulation* – "The Great Manipulation", but he has not published research because he was unable to prove the link between the mutilations and the UFO phenomenon. He does believe that the link exists, though.

Vallee finds the USAF's latest explanation of the Roswell incident – that it was the crash of a balloon carrying a basket full of mannequins – laughable.

'The most recent report from the Air Force is even more absurd than all the other "explanations" given previously,' he says. 'The fact that an extremely strange object came down near Roswell and that the military made every effort to discourage research into the incident and continues to do so is beyond doubt. However, this doesn't mean that the object in question was a UFO.'

For Vallee, the jury is still out on the Roswell incident. He believes that the idea of a crash is only plausible if you believe it to be a deliberate demonstration on the part of an external intelligence. In the meantime he is investigating nineteen other different crash cases.

Vallee believes that every country's armed forces uses the UFO phenomenon to cover up operations involving advanced or illegal weapons. This started in the USSR as early as 1967, when the KGB spread rumours about UFOs in a region where the inhabitants had seen rockets being launched that were carrying satellites in violation of international agreements. UFO rumours also cloak remotely controlled rigid airships that the military use to gather electromagnetic data. An American soldier he knows approached one of these craft standing in a clearing in Germany during manoeuvres before the Gulf War and he has read US patent applications describing them.

Generally Vallee's scientific colleagues are open-minded about UFOs. They have no time for grandiose conspiracy theories, but they do admit the existence of a 'non-standard phenomenon'. During his forty years of UFO investigations, he has discovered that the UFO phenomenon is considerably more complex than he used to think. It cannot be explained simply by an extrapolation of current human technology.

'We are faced with a phenomenon that underlies the whole of human history, manipulates the real world and seems to obey laws that bear no relationship to those we hitherto imagined,' he says. 'I believe we're entering a particularly exciting period in the phenomenon's history, since we now have the opportunity of re-examining all the various hypotheses.'

More recently, Vallee has published a memoir of his years in UFOlogy called *Science Interdite* (Forbidden Science). This also examines the validity of the US Army's secret 'Memorandum Pentacle'.

Bob Lazar

Soft-spoken physicist Bob Lazar is one of the most controversial figures UFOlogy. A man with a strong scientific background, he has been involved in the 'back-engineering' of alien spacecraft at the notorious Area 51 in the Nevada desert.

In 1982, he was a member of a scientific team at the US military's Groom Dry Lake installation. There he worked on a top-secret project to unravel the technology used by alien spacecraft that had been recovered from various crashes. Nine disc-shaped craft were held under armed guard in an underground section of the base known as 'S4'. The job of Lazar's team was to find out what made these flying saucers tick and whether their components could be replicated with materials found on Earth.

Many people have poured scorn on Lazar's story since it was first aired in a TV interview in 1989. As a child he was eccentric. His resumé includes bankruptcy and an association with a Las Vegas brothel. Lazar is easily discredited. Officials at Area 51 deny that anyone named Robert Lazar ever worked there – just as they once denied that Area 51 itself existed. But a salary statement issued by the United States Department of Naval Intelligence proves that Lazar did work at Area 51 for the five months as he claimed.

And when it comes to engineering, it is plain that Lazar knows what he is talking about. He has an impressive list of technical qualifications and is a scientist with a pedigree. In the early 1980s he was employed on several projects at the Los Alamos National Laboratory, in New Mexico, where the first atomic bomb was developed. At Los Alamos he conducted experiments with proton-scattering equipment and worked with high-energy particle accelerators. The work he did there was on the cutting edge of the new physics and could open the way to faster-than-light travel. As a prominent member of the town's scientific community, he earned himself an appearance on the front page of the *Los Alamos Monitor* when he installed a jet engine in a Honda CRX.

Despite the efforts made to paint him as slightly cracked, Lazar's account of what went on in Area 51 is lucid and concise, clearly not the ramblings of a disturbed mind. With his scientific background, his observations have a solid foundation. His specific task at Area 51 was to investigate the propulsion system of a small flying saucer dubbed 'the sports model', which was kept in one of the S4 hangars built into the side of a mountain. He witnessed a brief, low altitude test flight of the disc.

The sports model was some forty feet in diameter and fifteen feet high. It had three levels. The top level is an observation deck, nine feet across, with portholes. Below that were the control consoles and seats, which were too small and too near the floor for adult humans to use comfortably. The main cabin had a headroom of just six feet. Also in the central level was an antimatter reactor and, located directly below it on the lower level, were the three 'gravity amplifiers', connected to the reactor by wave guides. He worked on this propulsion system both in situ in the craft and on the bench in the lab.

The power source for the sports model and the eight other discs in S4 was an 'antimatter reactor', Lazar says. These reactors were fuelled by an orange-coloured, super-heavy material called 'Element 115'. This mysterious element was the source of the 'Gravity A' wave as yet undiscovered by terrestrial science. It also provided the antimatter radiation required to power the saucer in interstellar flight.

The flying saucers in S4 have two modes of travel. For local travel, near the surface of a planet, they use their gravity generators to balance the planet's gravitational field and ride a Gravity A wave like a cork on the ocean. During interstellar travel, covering distances that would take aeons even travelling at close to the speed of light, the Gravity A wave from the nucleus of Element 115 is amplified. This bends space and time in the same way it is bent in the intense gravitational field generated by a black hole. As the saucer travels through space, time is 'bent' around the craft. By distorting space and time in this manner, the disc can travel across vast expanses of space at incredible speeds. This is the same principle used by the *Enterprise*'s 'warp drive' in *Star Trek*.

Terrestrial rockets push the craft towards their destination by blasting jets of hot gas in the opposite direct, while alien craft 'pull' the destination towards them. Lazar explains how this works with the analogy of a rubber sheet with a stone, representing the spacecraft, on it. To go to any particular destination, you pinch the rubber sheet at that point and pull it towards the stone. Then, when you let got, the rubber sheet springs back, pulling the stone – or spacecraft with it.

'In a spacecraft that can exert a tremendous gravitational field by itself,' he says, 'you could sit in any particular place, turn on the gravity generator, and actually warp space and time and "fold" it. By shutting that off, you'd click back and you'd be at a tremendous distance from where you started.'

Although this type of propulsion appears to be the stuff of science fiction, many scientists believe that faster-than-light travel may be possible. Cambridge University's Lucasian professor of mathematics Stephen Hawking has suggested that interstellar travel might be achievable via natural or manmade 'worm-holes' in the fabric of space-time. Understanding how this works in practice is a bit more taxing, of course.

Inside the flying saucers' antimatter reactor, Lazar says, Element 115 is transmuted into another esoteric material called 'Element 116'. This is highly unstable and decays, releasing antimatter. The antimatter then reacts with matter inside the reactor in a total annihilation reaction, where one hundred per cent of the matter–antimatter is converted into energy. This energy is used to amplify the Gravity A wave given off the Element 115 and the heat generated by reaction is converted to electricity via a solid state thermo-electric generator.

The alien craft were saucer-shaped to diffuse the electrical charges generated by the antimatter reactor. In flight, Lazar says, the bottom of the alien craft glowed blue and began to hiss like a high voltage charge does on a sphere.

'It's my impression that the reason that they're round and have no sharp edges is to contain the high voltage,' says Lazar. 'If you've seen a high voltage system's insulators, things are round or else you get a corona discharge.'

The craft's high voltage makes them hiss when they take off. Otherwise they are silent. And the hissing stops when they have climbed to twenty or thirty feet. 'There are just too many things that Lazar knew about the discs that can't be explained in any other way,' said George Knapp, the TV journalist who first interviewed him.

Lazar says that, at one time, there were Soviet scientists and mathematicians working at Area 51, alongside the Americans there. He did not know whether they were actually allowed to work on the alien craft, but believes that they were employed on the scientific and mathematical theory that underpinned his group's practical work.

They were kicked out after a major breakthrough had been made in understanding how the discs and their propulsion systems worked. They were none too happy about this. Lazar says that in the aftermath of their exclusion, paranoia at the base soared. Employees were issued with firearms, in case the Soviets tried to kidnap them.

During his time at Area 51, Lazar had to read a document the size of a telephone directory, which revealed that the top-secret base at Groom Lake was not the only US government facility back-engineering ET technology. The US government's admission that other secret bases do exist lent weight to Lazar's story. However, what goes on in them is still beyond top secret. Since Lazar's Area 51 security clearance was mysteriously revoked at the end of the 1980s, he has been subjected of intense harassment. His house and car have been broken into and he has been shot at by unseen snipers in an attempt to discourage him from divulging the secrets of S4.

Edgar Fouche

Like Bob Lazar, Edgar Fouche worked at Area 51 and has since spent his time telling the world about what is going on there. Fouche is a true insider who spent twenty-eight years with the US Air Force and Department of Defense. During that time, he was stationed at top-secret sites, including the nuclear test site in Nevada, the Nellis Test Range and the Groom Lake Air Base, home of Area 51. Fouche's work in intelligence, electronics, communications and a number of black programmes has given him inside information on some of America's most classified technological developments, including the super-secret SR-71 and SR-75 spy planes and the TR-3B, which many people believe is sometimes mistake for the Flying Triangle.

However, during the 1980s when President Reagan was in power, he became completely disenchanted with the defence industry. It was full of fraud and abuse of power and he decided that he could not be associated with it anymore. He was suffering serious medical problems at the time and did not think he was going to live much longer. So he decided to speak up.

In this, he was helped by five friends who served with him in Vietnam. One was a former SR-71 spy plane pilot. Two of them went on to work for the National Security Agency. A fourth friend's father had worked for the NSA for twenty years and the fifth worked for the Department of Defense. He also gleaned information about the TR-3B by talking to pilots.

His buddy who was the SR-71 pilot told him that once, when he was flying back across the South China Sea, he saw a shadow fall across the cockpit. The aircraft started to nose down and the avionics went crazy. When he looked up to find out what was happening, he saw a UFO that was so big it completely blocked out the sun. It was oval and was surrounded by a shimmering energy field, and he reckoned that it was three hundred feet across.

What really amazed Fouche was that all the pilots he spoke to reported encounters with UFOs. Some had seen circular UFOs, others had encountered plasma balls that seemed to dance around the craft. These reports were all the more impressive because the SR-71 can fly at over 60,000 feet. This gives it enormous visibility. If something is up there, an SR-71 is going to see it.

Fouche's contacts told him that the development of the TR-3B started in 1982 as part of a top-secret project named 'Aurora', whose aim was to build and test advanced aerospace vehicles. He discovered that around 35 per cent of the US government's 'Star Wars' budget had been siphoned off to finance it. The TR-3B is a triangular nuclear-powered aerospace platform and is undoubtedly the most exotic aerospace programme in existence. It designation 'TR' stands for tactical reconnaissance. This means the craft is designed to get to the target and stay there long enough pick up information on the enemy's deployment and send it back. The advantage of being powered by a nuclear reactor is that it can stay aloft for a long time without refuelling.

Its advanced propulsion system also allows it to hover silently for long periods. The circular crew compartment is located at the centre of TR-3B's triangular airframe. It is surrounded by a plasma-filled accelerator ring, called the Magnetic Field Disrupter, which generates a magnetic vortex and neutralises the pull of gravity. The MFD does not actually power the craft; what it does is effectively reduce its mass. Propulsion is achieved by three multimode gas-propelled thrusters mounted on each corner of the triangle. But the MFD makes the aircraft incredibly light. It can fly at Mach 9 speeds vertically and horizontally, and can outmanoeuvre anything except UFOs.

One of Fouche's sources who worked on the TR-3B told him that they were working on the possibility of developing the MFD technology so that it not only reduces mass but also creates a force that repels gravity. This would give the TR-3B a propulsion system that would allow it to fly routinely to the moon or Mars. This antigravity system is how UFOs work and Fouche is convinced that the TR-3B has been developed through the back-engineering of alien technology.

Fouche believes that the black triangles tracked by the Belgian Air Force in the late 1980s and early 1990s were TR-3Bs. He has a simple rule: if it is triangular it is terrestrial, if it is circular or tubular it is extraterrestrial. He says that the US government could easily get round treaty agreements that prohibit testing advanced aircraft over Europe. These agreements, he points out, say that they cannot fly an aircraft over a friendly country without that country being informed. It would be easy enough to inform the Belgian government on the sly. After all, the US is not supposed to have nuclear weapons in the UK or Japan, but they do.

Groom Lake's six-mile-long runway is the longest in the world. Fouche says that it was built to accommodate the CIA's latest super-hi-tech spy plane, the 'Penetrator' or SR-75; 'SR' stands for strategic reconnaissance. It can exceed Mach 7 with speeds of over 28,000 miles an hour at an altitude of 40,000 feet and can reach any point on the Earth within three hours. This plane is so secret that the US government does not even admit to its existence. After the SR-71 Blackbird was retired in 1990, the US Air Force said that it would not be replaced because satellites provided all the military's high-level reconnaissance needs. But Fouche's sources say that the SR-75 has been designed to service spy satellites in orbit. It acts as a 'mothership' and launches unmanned SR-74, or Scramp, craft. Operated by remote control, these can place satellites in space, reaching altitudes of 95 miles and speeds of 6,250 miles an hour, or Mach 15.

Fouche was assigned to Groom Lake in 1979 because he was one of the few people who had the necessary top-secret clearance. He was certified to work with particular equipment which, even years after the event, he was not prepared to discuss. He had been working at Nellis Air Force Base at the time and was told that he was being temporarily reassigned, but was given no idea of where he was going to be sent. Some thirty technicians were herded onto a blue bus with blacked-out windows. There were two guards on board, armed with M16 rifles. They told the passengers not to speak unless spoken to. This is how Fouche ended up at Groom Lake.

The conditions were extremely oppressive. He was issued with heavy glasses, like welders' goggles. These had thick lenses that blocked peripheral vision and prevented the wearer from seeing more than thirty metres ahead. Everywhere he went, he was escorted by a soldier carrying an M16 who would never talk to him. He could not even go to the lavatory alone.

According to Fouche, the military used sinister mind-control techniques on employees. One of his five collaborators named Sal was a victim of this. A former NSA electronic intelligence expert, he had helped develop Magnetic Field Disruption. After two-years at a top-secret NSA facility, he came down with what he thought was the flu. He went to see the facility's doctor, who gave him some medication and told him to go home and rest. The next day, Sal had no memory of where he worked or who he worked for. When his brother contacted the NSA, he was told that Sal's contract had been terminated. Sal's memory has not returned and the only evidence he has that he worked at the NSA facility at all is a few scribbled notes and his pay slips.

Security at Area 51 was so tight that a key card and a code were needed for every door. Fouche is very sceptical about people who claim to have been at Groom Lake and accidentally stumbled into a hangar with a UFO inside. His twenty-eight years with the Department of Defense and the US Air Force taught him that anything that was top-secret was protected by numerous levels of security.

However, in Area 51 there is a facility on the Papoose Lake site called the Defense Advanced Research Center, which extends for ten storeys underground. It was built in the early 1980s with Strategic Defense Initiative money. The DARC is the centre for what is officially designated 'Foreign Artefacts' – this means alien artefacts. Crashed and recovered alien technology is stored there. The DARC is where all the analysis of 'extraterrestrial biological entities' – alien creatures – and back-engineering takes place.

Fouche says that the reason the US government cannot come clean about what they are up to at Area 51 is because, since the birth of the UFO phenomenon in 1947, it has consistently violated people's constitutional rights. The government considers anything that it cannot control a threat, he says. It cannot control the alien agenda, so it tries to control any information surrounding it. People who find out too much about UFOs or aliens either disappear or have been killed, he says. The government would be held accountable if the facts got out and it could not handle that.

David Adair

Another witness to what is going on at Area 51 is space scientist David Adair. He became involved in the world of UFOs through his lifelong passion for science and rocketry.

Adair was a child prodigy. He built his first rocket at the age of eleven. This was no fourth-of-July firework. He fashioned it from sophisticated alloys, using tools and fuels from his father's machine shop.

Then, in 1968, he set out to build a new type of rocket which used powerful electromagnetic fields to contain and harness the thermonuclear energy from a fusion reaction. Although this sounds exotic, it was not his original idea. He got the plans from the long-range planning division of NASA's Marshall Space Flight Center in Huntsville, Alabama. They had come up with the theoretical designs for fifty different types of engine. Only two of them used conventional liquid fuel or solid propellants, so fusion was the obvious way to go. The one that Adair decided to build was a remarkable design. At the time he wondered why NASA had never made it themselves. Later he realised that they probably chose not to develop it for political reasons. If you developed an efficient fusion-based propulsion system, oil and gas would be redundant. Nevertheless, the fourteen-year-old Adair saw the design's potential and, through Republican Congressman John Ashbrook, he got a $1-million grant to build it.

But the grant came with strings attached. The Department of Defense were involved. He was prohibited from telling anyone about what he was building. And for Adair the outside world ceased to exist as he worked on the rocket day and night for the next three years. In 1971, when Adair was seventeen, the rocket was ready to be tested. General Curtis LeMay, the project manager, decided that the rocket was too powerful to be tested outside a secure military facility, so he scheduled a test at White Sands Missile Range in New Mexico.

When Adair was at White Sands preparing for the test, a black DC-9 arrived. It was carrying Dr Arthur Rudolph, one of the designers of the Saturn-5 moon rocket. Originally Rudolph had worked on the Nazi German V-2 programme, but after the war had been taken to America. Adair told Rudolph that, proportionately, his rocket was a thousand times more powerful than the Saturn-5, and Rudolph was furious.

When Adair was programming his rocket's guidance system, his military bosses gave him a precise location for the landing. The co-ordinates they gave him specified a place four hundred miles away in an area called Groom Lake in Nevada. This puzzled Adair as all the maps showed there was an empty dry lake bed.

After the rocket was launched successfully, Adair was told to get on board the DC-9. They flew him to Groom Lake and, as they came in to land, he could see the huge runways and a huge base that had not appeared on the map. This, he was informed, was Area 51.

When he arrived at Groom Lake, Adair thought he was there to collect his rocket. But he was bundled onto an electric golf cart and driven over to three large hangars. As he got close to the buildings, he could see that they were new, but they had been painted to look much older. The middle hangar was the area of two football fields. Once he was inside, warning lights began flashing, guard rails sprang up and an area of the floor about seven hundred square feet started to descend. Adair realised they were on a huge lift. It went down through solid rock and, when it stopped, Adair found himself in the biggest underground space he had ever seen. It contained a lot of aircraft. Most of them were covered up, but he recognised one as the XB-70, an experimental aircraft. It was huge. But he also noticed a number of craft that were a strange teardrop shape with their surfaces perfectly smooth in all directions. The most peculiar thing about them was that they did not have any of the intake or exhaust ports that are needed by jet engines. In fact, they had no visible means of propulsion, yet they were surrounded by support equipment and looked quite capable of flying. Looking back, he now thinks that they used some kind of electromagnetic or flux-field propulsion.

Still in the golf cart, he was driven over to a big set of doors. The driver jumped out and put his hand on a panel. It flashed and the doors opened. We know these things now as optical hand-print scanners, but in 1971 they were the stuff of science fiction. Inside the air was cold and the lighting was strange. There was plenty of light, but nothing seemed to cast a shadow. He was then shown a huge engine that was about the size of a bus. It looked like two octopuses linked together by their tentacles. When Adair examined it, he realised it was some kind of giant version of the motor in his rocket.

His companions explained that this engine used a fusion reaction similar the one he had designed and they wanted his opinion on the firing mechanism. The whole situation struck Adair as bizarre. Why didn't they ask the people who built it, he enquired. He was told they were on leave. So Adair asked to look at their design notes. This seemed to annoy the people who had brought him there.

'Look son, do you want to help your country or not?' they said.

Adair believes that the engine was extraterrestrial in origin. Although it was huge, he could not see a single bolt, rivet or screw holding it together. The surface was perfectly smooth and, although the room was cold, it felt warm to the touch. Whenever he touched the surface, bluish white waves swirled out from his hands and disappeared into the material. They would stop each time he moved his hand away. He climbed up on top of the engine and looked inside. He saw a large container holding bundles of tubes. These were filled with some kind of liquid. Adair's overall impression was that it was organic – part mechanical, part biological. He realised it had been made using non-terrestrial techniques and materials.

He shrugged his shoulders and told his companions that he had no idea how the thing worked. The manufacturing techniques used were very different from anything he had ever seen before. He reasoned that it could not have been built by American engineers or by the Soviets. As it dawned on him that it must have been built using extraterrestrial technology, he got angry. Flying saucers had landed and the government were keeping it a secret. When Adair expressed his outrage at this, his companions shouted at him to get away from the device.

Adair does not think that the engine was working too well, though they have had three decades to work on it since then and he hopes they have been successful. He could certainly see the potential. Adair's own rocket was puny by comparison but it channelled enormous amounts of energy out of the back of the rocket for propulsion. He believes that the alien engine could have managed to contain all the incredible energy generated by the fusion reaction inside the propulsion system, producing a 'field effect' outside the craft. This would create a huge 'gravitation well' which would break through the fabric of space-time. Space would be folded back on itself, allowing the craft to travel vast distances in an instant, without exceeding the speed of light.

However, he is still angry that this device and other exotic craft are in government hands and all their amazing technology is hidden from the rest of the world. Meanwhile people at NASA are struggling to send small spacecraft to Mars. The fact that the US government are withholding knowledge of their contact with other civilisations he also finds incredible.

'These are ET civilisations we could learn so much from,' Adair says. 'When I think of all the ways that we could advance with this knowledge of ET contact, it makes me sick that this information is hidden.'

Since his visit to Area 51 in 1971, Adair has worked as a technology transfer consultant, redesigning space-programme technology for commercial applications. He has an office in Ventura, California. But he has not forgotten what he saw.

On 9 April 1997, Adair testified to a Congressional hearing in Washington, D.C. as part of the campaign for full UFO disclosure. The hearings were organised by the Center for the Study of Extraterrestrial Intelligence and gave key witnesses, including military personnel and pilots, the opportunity to lobby the US government. David Adair was under oath when he told the Congressional panel what he had seen in Area 51 and, unexpectedly, the Congressmen immediately got confirmation that he was telling the truth.

During his testimony, Adair mentioned that the device he had seen was covered in strange markings. He remembered what they looked like and drew them for the panel. Also giving testimony was an attorney from North Carolina named Steven Lovekin, who had top-secret clearance when he worked as a cryptologist at the Pentagon in the 1950s. As military aide, he had given regular briefings to President Eisenhower on UFO activity. In that capacity, he had been shown a piece of metal that he was told came from a downed flying saucer. It was covered in strange markings – the same markings Adair had seen in Area 51.

Wendelle Stevens

Wendelle Stevens' involvement with UFOs began in 1947 when he was assigned to the Air Technical Intelligence Center at Wright Field in Dayton, Ohio, home to the USAF's various in-house UFO study programmes, Sign, Grudge and Blue Book. That year, Stevens was sent from Ohio to Alaska to supervise a squadron of B-29 bombers that were being used to map the Arctic. However, he discovered there was a hidden agenda behind their polar mission. The B-29s were equipped with cutting-edge electronic detection technology and cameras to detect and film 'foo fighters' as UFOs were then known.

Stevens's security clearance was not high enough to allow him to see the footage the B-29s had shot before it was sent to Washington, but the pilots told him of their UFO encounters. Many of his pilots saw UFOs soar rapidly into the sky and fly off as the B-29s approached. In most cases, they caused electromagnetic disturbances to the plane's instrumentation, often affecting the engines. On one occasion a UFO approached a B-29 head on. Then, before they collided, it slammed into reverse, manoeuvred itself around next to the wing and stayed there.

Astounded by these revelations, Stevens asked his superiors if he could pursue an investigation into the UFO phenomenon. He was told he could do so only outside of official military channels. So, in 1963, after twenty-three years' active service, he retired and began a new career as a UFO researcher.

He began collecting newspaper clippings of UFOs from all over the world. Where photographs had been printed, he would write to the people who had taken them and ask for a copy. Now he boasts the world's largest collection of UFO photographs – over three thousand images in all – along with a vast library of UFO film and videos.

To establish the authenticity of the photographs, he visits the person who took it and investigates their encounter. He also examines their camera equipment and takes his own photographs from the same spot, so that he can compare relative scale and distances. After these preliminary checks, he subjects the photograph to a series of analytical procedures. Today he uses computer techniques. It was easier in the old days, he says, when all a photographic expert had to do was to make large-scale blow-up and examine it with a magnifying glass.

Stevens is one of the few UFOlogists who has made a career of studying contactees. In 1976 he was the first researcher to investigate the claims of Swiss contactee Eduard 'Billy' Meier, who was in telepathic contact with aliens and photographed their spaceships coming into land. At Stevens' behest, Meier submitted his evidence for analysis to scientists at McDonnell Douglas, IBM and NASA's Jet Propulsion Laboratory. Their results were inconclusive. However, computer analysis of one of Meier's pictures reveals a model next to a fake tree and models of flying saucers were found in Meier's home. Nonetheless, Stevens believes Meier is genuine.

Stevens decided to specialise in contactees because they presented a unique opportunity to learn about extraterrestrials and their possible agendas. If possible he sets up a two-way dialogue, asking contactees to pose questions to the extraterrestrials for him next time they meet. Sometimes he gets an answer.

One of the most important contactee cases he investigated was that of Bill Herrmann, who lived in Charleston, South Carolina, near the Air Force base there. He and his wife repeatedly saw a UFO, which flew in a darting motion with sharp, angular turns, unlike the smooth turns of a plane. One night in 1977, when he was trying to get a closer look at it through binoculars, Herrmann was abducted. He was enveloped in a beam of blue light, which drew him up inside the UFO. The extraterrestrials he encountered inside the craft were friendly. They came from one of the twin stars in the Reticulum system. When he asked them questions, he would hear their replies in English inside his head. They told him that the darting movements of their craft were made to avoid any radar lock-on. Radar-guided weapons had previously been responsible for the crashes of three of their ships. They also told Herrmann that they wanted their downed ships back and were prepared to negotiate, but the US government was too hostile to deal with. After this first abduction experience, Herrmann was invited back onto the craft another five times.

When Stevens began investigating the Herrmann case, he discovered that the Reticulans were sending Herrmann vast amounts of information when he was in a trance-like state. He transcribed the transmission in automatic writing. The result was numerous pages of text in a totally unknown alphabet, along with schematic diagrams of their propulsion system. The complex technical information he was provided with was way beyond current human scientific knowledge and Herrmann could never have acquired it from any terrestrial source.

From his work with contactees, Stevens has discovered that there are many different kinds of extraterrestrial. They come from different places and have different languages, morphologies, technologies and agendas. The largest group are the various humanoid species who often tell contactees that they come from the Pleiades star system. The next largest group are the well-known 'Greys', which again comprise a number of different races.

Stevens has also carried out research on Area 51 and tracked down Derek Hennesy, a former security guard who worked on level two of S4, the famous underground complex where Lazar had worked on alien propulsion systems. During his time there,

Hennesy saw nine bays for flying saucer bays on level one. There were a further seven bays on level two with three identical alien craft in the first three bays. Hennesy also saw large tubes that contained the preserved bodies of dead Greys. After Stevens first interviewed Hennesy, Hennesy disappeared for a while. When he re-emerged he claimed to have no knowledge of what he had previously seen or said.

However, Stevens had another friend who works as an engineer at Area 51 and says it is engaged in bridging the gap between alien technology and our own. He has built simulators to train human pilots to fly flying saucers. There are two extraterrestrials at Area 51 who can fly alien craft. They have been trying to train humans to do this, but not very successfully. So far they are limited to flights within the atmosphere. They have not yet mastered flight in deep space, but they can hover using some kind of gravity propulsion.

Stevens thinks that there is little chance that the curtain of official secrecy surrounding UFOs will be lifted in the near future. The government have kept what they know a secret for fifty years and he expects them to do so for another fifty. Governments have far too much to lose from any official disclosure, he reckons. The impact on society would be incalculable. The only way the world's governments would admit to the reality of alien visitations is if a group of extraterrestrials makes its presence visible on a massive scale, he says. Stevens believes that there are signs that this may be about to occur in Mexico, where there was an explosion in the number of sightings in the 1990s.

Peter Gersten

For twenty years, New York criminal defence attorney Peter Gersten specialised in murder and drug cases. But then, in 1977, as the lawyer for the UFO group Ground Saucer Watch, he took the CIA to court and won. It was a historic victory for UFOlogy.

The suit was filed under the Freedom of Information Act. Ground Saucer Watch were trying to force the CIA to release just five UFO-related documents the agency had in its possession. But

Gersten expanded the case. Under the FOIA it was as easy to create a lawsuit to get the CIA to release all the UFO document it had as it was to get just five. As a result, in 1979, the CIA was forced to release nine hundred pages of UFO-related documents – the first time that any US intelligence agency had ever released previously classified UFO information to the public. A further fifty-seven documents were withheld. But the case showed beyond any doubt that the CIA, which had previously denied any involvement in UFOs, had been studying them for years.

The documents not only confirmed the reality of UFOs and gave detailed descriptions of them, they also gave researchers access to numerous reports from credible witnesses – scientists, military personnel and law enforcement officers. Some of the documents released originated from other agencies. This confirmed that every other US agency had also been studying the UFO phenomenon and that the military had been involved in UFO research even before 1947.

Bolstered by this success, Gersten formed Citizens Against UFO Secrecy (CAUS), an organisation dedicated to breaking down the wall of secrecy surrounding the UFO phenomenon. Its aim is to force the government to come clean on what it knows about contact with extraterrestrial intelligence, and it believes that the public has the absolute and unconditional right to know.

In the early 1980s, Gersten continued his legal assault on the US intelligence community, taking the National Security Agency to court after the NSA refused an FOIA request for UFO-related documents that CAUS knew they had in their possession. In court, the judge asked the NSA's attorney how many documents had surfaced when they had processed the CAUS's FOIA request. He was told that it was classified information. Gersten told the judge that the CIA had told him that the NSA had at least eighteen documents. The judge then insisted that the NSA come up with a figure. The agency finally admitted that there were 135. But that was as far as it went. The NSA invoked the National Security Exemption, one of twelve exemption clauses built into the FOIA. To argue their exemption, the NSA used a twenty-one-page affidavit that was itself classified, and the case was dismissed.

Although Gersten was unsuccessful in obtaining the UFO documents, he did succeed in getting the NSA to admit that they held them. He took the appeal to the Supreme Court and, when it was dismissed, it made headline news. Even though he did not get the documents, he had succeeded in drawing great attention to the issue of UFO secrecy and highlighted the US Supreme Court's role in this cover-up.

In further court actions, Gersten succeed in forcing the release of a heavily censored version of the NSA exemption affidavit and, in due course, most of the documents they withheld have been released.

Gersten is not optimistic about the efforts of various organisations – such as Dr Steven Greer's Center for the Study of Extraterrestrial Intelligence – to get US Congress to hold open hearings on the subject of UFOs. He says that the idea of open hearings is inherently ridiculous because any discussion of UFOs involves a discussion of advanced technology. This is an area that the military keeps secret by invoking national security, while the corporations protect their developments by using patents. The elected officials of Congress are always up for re-election – every two years for Representatives and six years for Senators. They need money and are always vulnerable to the demands of special interests.

Getting Congress to grant immunity to people who may have to break secrecy oaths to testify would not help. Gersten points out the problems: 'Let's say you have a general who wants to testify in a Congressional hearing even though he is sworn to secrecy. He will naturally expect Congress to grant him immunity. However, the military will then question Congress's right to grant immunity and they would then have to fight it out in the courts, which could take years.'

Gersten finds it more effective to work through CAUS where he can protect the privacy of any informant, through client–attorney privilege, at the same time getting the information out.

He used the Freedom of Information Act to try and pressurise the US Army into releasing documents relating to statements made by Colonel Philip J. Corso in his book, *The Day After Roswell.* Corso was willing to testify that he had seen the bodies of dead aliens in 1947 and that he had read alien autopsy reports in 1961. Gersten was ready to take the issue to court, so he filed a FOIA request with the US Army for the release of any documents they may have had supporting Corso's claims. The Army claimed it could find no documents and Gersten took them to court. But Corso died and, on 26 April 1999, the case was dismissed. Gersten decided not to take that matter any further. Instead, he filed a suit against the Department of Defense over Flying Triangles, in an attempt to find out what these mysterious craft actually are. While Gersten concedes that some of the sighting reports clearly describe advanced US experimental aircraft such as the TR-3B, which researcher Ed Fouche claims was built at Area 51, many of the reports could not possibly be the TR-3B. People have seen triangular craft that are half-a-mile wide. Some are seen at treetop level and over populated areas, shining beams of light on the ground. Witnesses also report seeing orb-shaped lights detach from these craft, fly around and re-attach. None of this can be explained in terms of advanced military technology.

Gersten sued the US government for damages after Betty Cash, Vickie Landrum and her grandson were abducted in Texas on the night of 29 December 1980. Gersten argued that as the UFO concerned was escorted by twenty Chinook helicopters it must have been part of a military operation. The case was dismissed on the grounds that the government denied all knowledge of the UFO and Gersten could not prove that it belonged to them.

Gersten is also bringing a unprecedented FOIA lawsuit against the CIA, the FBI and Department of Defense on the grounds that alien abduction can be viewed legally as a form of invasion. Article 4, section 4 of the US Constitution requires that the Federal Government protect the individual states against invasion, a provision that was enacted to persuade the original colonies to abandon their independent militias and join the Union. However, the Federal government are plainly failing in their duty to protect citizens of the States if those citizens are being abducted.

CAUS and Gersten have even more ambitious plans. Because it is unlikely that the President is going to open up all the files on UFOs in the foreseeable future, they want to find out for themselves. They are planning a privately funded mission to the Moon, and hope to be able to send back pictures from the Sinu Medi regions where some UFOlogists have located alien structures. Using existing technology, they estimate that their 'Project Destination Moon' would cost $12 million – small change to the likes of Bill Gates and Ted Turner.

'Think of all the money sponsors would make from the publicity if they funded the first civilian mission to the moon, especially if alien artefacts were discovered,' says the ever-optimistic Gersten. 'The space programme is in the hands of the government and the military. We are all like virtual prisoners on this planet. This is a project that is just waiting to happen.'

Derrel Sims

Alien implant expert Derrel Sims is a former CIA operative who got involved in UFO research after being abducted himself. He has conscious recollections of multiple abductions between the ages of three and seventeen.

He started researching in this field when he was sixteen years old and has been at it for more than twenty-seven years. After leaving the world of covert intelligence, he rose to become chief of investigation for the Houston-based Fund for Interactive Research and Space Technology, where he concentrated on collecting physical evidence, as he believes that this is the best way to prove that UFOs and alien abductions actually exist.

He has investigated hundreds of cases of alien implants, some of which have been inside the body for up to forty-one years. Despite being foreign bodies, they trigger no inflammatory response. He says that the devices found are 'meteoric' in origin. Although some labs have said that this is impossible, 'double blind' tests have proved this to be the case.

Dr Roger Leir

For years, people doubted the reality of alien abductions. This was largely because abductees had no physical evidence to back their stories. One man changed all that – Dr Roger Leir. A podiatrist from south California, he was the first doctor surgically to remove an alien implant. Until his first operation in August 1995, they had been seen only on X-rays and CAT scans.

Leir had a long interest in UFOs and was a long-standing member of the Mutual UFO Network, where he gained an investigator's certificate. As an investigator, he attended a UFO conference in Los Angeles in June 1995, when he met Derrel Sims. Sims showed Leir a number of X-rays. One of them showed a foreign object in the big toe of an abductee. Leir was sceptical, but Derrel produced the abductee's medical records, which showed that she had never had surgery on her foot. Leir offered to remove it and this led to a series of operations on abductees.

He selects candidates for surgery by strict criteria, which were developed when Leir was working at the National Institute for Discovery Science. Anyone undergoing surgery had to be a suspected abductee – they had to have experienced missing time or, at the very least, seen a UFO. They had to fill out a form that determined how deeply they were involved in the abduction phenomenon. They also had to have an object in their body that showed up on an X-ray, CAT scan or MRI.

Some of Leir's patients have a conscious memory of the object being implanted into their bodies during the abduction, but more often, implants are discovered by accident. Some abductees find unusual lumps and scars that have suddenly appeared and go to their doctors to get them X-rayed. In one case, an implant was discovered during treatment following a car crash. All Leir's patients are given a psychological examination before and after the implant is removed. Some of them experience a new-found sense of freedom after surgery. One abductee went straight back to her family, saying she wanted nothing more to do with UFOs.

Leir has, so far, operated on eight individuals and removed a total of nine objects. Seven of them seem to be of extraterrestrial origin. Five were coated in a dark grey shiny membrane that was impossible to cut through even with a brand new surgical blade. One was T-shaped. Another three were greyish-white balls that were attached to an abnormal area of the skin. Leir found that patients would react violently if the object was touched and often suffered pain in that area in the week before the implant was surgically removed.

During surgery, Leir discovered that there was no inflammatory response in the flesh around the implant. He found this surprising as any foreign object introduced into the body usually causes an inflammatory response. In this case, there was no rejection. He also found that the surrounding tissue also contained large numbers of 'proprioceptors'. These are specialised nerve cells usually found in sensitive areas, such the finger tips, which sense temperature, pressure and touch. There was no medical reason for them to found where he found them, clustered around the implant. In two cases, Leir found 'scoop mark' lesions above the implants. In each case, Leir found that the tissue there suffered from a condition called 'solar elastosis'. This is caused by exposure to ultraviolet light, but it could not have been due to sunburn as only a tiny area was affected.

Leir found that the membrane surrounding the implants was composed of protein coagulum, hemosiderin granules – an iron pigment – and keratin. All these three substances are found naturally in the body. However, a search of the medical literature revealed that they had never been found together in combination before.

The implants themselves would fluoresce under ultraviolet light – usually green, but sometimes other colours. In one case, Leir found that an abductee had a pink stain on the palm of her hand. It could be removed temporarily, but would seep back under the skin. Derrel Sims uses this fluorescent staining, which cannot be removed by washing, to detect implants. Leir believes that it is caused by a substance given off by the implant to prevent rejection.

A wide range of tests have been carried out on the implants Leir has removed. They are submitted to routine pathology tests to see if they are human in origin. When that draws a blank, they are sent for metallurgical testing and they have been examined under optical microscopes and electron microscopes, and analysed using X-ray diffraction techniques that tell which elements they are made of.

When the T-shaped implant that Leir had removed from one patient was magnified one thousand times under an electron microscope, a tiny fishhook could be seen on one end of the crossbar of the T, which Leir believes anchored the implant to the flesh. The other end was rounded off like the nose of a bullet, while in the middle there was a tiny hole into which the shaft of the T fitted perfectly. One of the rods had a carbon core, which made it electrically conductive. The other had an iron core, which was magnetic. An attractive force between them made them cling together. The shaft was encircled by a band of silicate crystals. Bob Beckworth, an electrical engineer who works with Leir, likened this to an old-fashioned crystal set, where a quartz crystal and a copper wire were used to pick up a radio signal.

Specimens were sent to some of the most prestigious laboratories in North America – Los Alamos National Laboratories, New Mexico Tech and Toronto University, among others. The samples were found to contain rare elements in the same isotopic ratios that are found in meteorites. When the labs were told that the specimens had been removed from body tissue, they did not believe it. For Leir, this is the smoking gun.

When you mine an element on Earth, the ratio of the various radioactive isotopes it contains always falls within a certain range. If you mine uranium, for example, it will always contain a certain ratio of uranium 234, 235 and 236. This will be roughly the same anywhere on Earth. But rock samples from the moon or meteorites contain completely different isotopic ratios. The isotopic ratios in the implants showed clearly that they were not of earthly origin.

Leir is not sure what the implants are for. They could be transponders or locating devices that enable alien abductors to track those they have abducted. They might be designed to modify behaviour – some abductees exhibit unexplained compulsive behaviour. They might detect chemical changes in the body, caused by pollution. Or they may be used to detect genetic changes in the body.

'If researchers such as Zachariah Sitchen are correct,' says Leir, 'and the human race is a genetically-altered species, then it's possible that this genetic manipulation may still be going on and is something "they" wish to monitor closely.'

But whatever implants are for, it is quite clear that they are extraterrestrial in origin. As Leir points out, if you find people who have been abducted by aliens and then find implants in them that have an isotopic ratio not found this planet, what other sane conclusion can you draw?

Tony Dodd

Ex-Sergeant Tony Dodd became interested in UFOs after having an encounter with one himself in 1978, when he was a police officer in North Yorkshire. He saw an object hovering about a hundred feet away. It had a domed top with four doors it. There were flashing lights around the sides, and three large spheres protruding from the underside. The whole structure was glowing bright white and it was silent. Dodd was sure this strange object was homing in on him, though it eventually floated off and landed nearby.

After he reported his sighting, his superiors told him not to talk to the press. This was standard procedure in the police.

Since then, he has seen seventy or eighty UFOs. Some of them are simply balls of light, anything from a couple of feet to thirty feet across. However, they seemed to contain some kind of mechanical device. He could often see a small, red pulse of light inside them, which created the aura of light. He has received hundreds of reports of these balls of light, which apparently fly in formation. That must mean they have intelligent controls, he reasons.

After retiring from the police force, Dodd took the opportunity to speak out. He devoted himself to UFO research full-time and became Director of Investigative Services for Quest International, one of the world's leading UFO societies, and he oversees the publication of their high influential *UFO Magazine*. For part of his time in the police, he was a detective and he uses police investigation techniques on UFO cases. His police background has taught him which lines of enquiry to pursue and how to encourage witnesses to come forward and talk. It has also given him contacts in intelligence and the military. This is not always an advantage. Dodd's mail is tampered with, even the registered packages that turn up. And the CIA have threatened to kill him, though he remains stoically unintimidated.

Dodd is the foremost expert on animal mutilations in the UK and believes the government know all about it. He also believes that elite forces in America and Britain adopted a hostile attitude towards a certain type of alien because the aliens out there do not resemble us very closely. Aliens, he points out, do not necessarily have two legs and two arms. Indeed, in human eyes some are quite grotesque. This is the reason the aliens are abducting people and creating hybrids. The aliens, apparently feel the same way about us. When people are abducted, they are treated the way we treat animals on game reserves.

Abductions are never one-off incidents, he says. Dodd has never come across a victim who has been abducted in childhood and never abducted again. Once it has happened, it tends to occur throughout the victim's life. Dodd believes that abductees are being conditioned until they reach puberty. After that the visitors start taking sperm and eggs. Part of the aliens' agenda, Dodd believes, is a genetic experiment to create human–alien hybrids. He has investigated cases where aliens have impregnated female abductees. The conception is not natural. It is performed with a needle that it inserted through the navel. Human babies can be conceived using similar methods, but our medical profession is years behind. Three months into the pregnancy, the abductee is picked up again and the foetus is taken from the womb. The resulting 'star children' have thin limbs, large heads and alien eyes and faces, though they have hair on their heads and small human noses.

One woman he knows has been impregnated twice and both times the aliens have taken the baby. When the woman was three months pregnant, she was out walking her dog and a strange light appeared in the sky. She knew they had come to take her baby. She also saw jars containing embryos, which were suspended in liquid, as if in an artificial womb. These jars were all around the walls of the room she was in.

In many of the cases that Dodd has investigated, the abductees seem to have a sixth sense that makes them aware that the abduction is about to take place. However, people generally do not know that they have been abducted, and the clue is when they know things that they would not normally know about.

He uses lie detectors in his investigations. But he also uses his knowledge of the subject and his police background to sniff out the hoaxers. He also uses hypnosis and always employs the same hypnotist. This is because the man does nothing more than put the subject under hypnosis. Dodd himself asks all the questions. This is vital because he does not want the witnesses to be led or have them given guides or pointers.

In abduction cases, Dodd also looks for physical evidence. Some abductees have strange marks on their bodies. In one case he investigated, a woman saw strange balls of light in the bedroom at night, and she had an inexplicable burn mark on her arm. The woman had contacted him after he had made a radio broadcast about alien abductions and, although many of the things he had mentioned had happened to her, she wanted to be reassured that she had not been abducted.

He has also come across a case where an abductee set off a camera flash near an alien implant in his head. Something under his skin glowed green. It was about a quarter of an inch wide, but it did not seem to cause the man any pain.

On several occasions, Dodd has had a person under hypnosis who has ended up speaking as somebody else – one of the aliens, Dodd believes. When he asked them what right they had to abduct people, the alien voice replied: 'We have every right to do this, you do not understand the nature of things.' Dodd concluded that he was talking to a highly intelligent being.

Dodd has tried to develop this as a method of communication with the alien race and has come to believe that extra-terrestrial beings are involved in a collect-and-analyse experiment to study the human race. He is in regular communication with them, but they only divulge things piece by piece. When he gets impatient, they tell him that they have to take things slowly because a human race is not able to handle the truth. We have to be educated as if we are in infant school. Dodd finds this very spiritual.

This is why they are not communicating with all of us. We are not ready for the knowledge they possess. That is why Dodd himself is here. His role is to disseminate information, to learn from the aliens and to give what he knows out to humankind. His alien contacts have told him that he is some form of teacher. Apparently this was decided before he arrived on Earth as a child and it is why they are making contact with him. They have explained humankind's place in the universe and have told him that we are immortal spirits that go on and on.

'Every flower has its seed and every creature its destiny,' Dodd has been told, 'weep not for those who have fulfilled their earthly obligation, but be happy that they have escaped that charge of material suffering. As the flower dies, the seed is born and so shall it be for all things.'

Dodd's contact with the aliens has religious aspects. He believes they are a higher force and that they are responsible for us being here.

A.J. Gevaerd

A. J. Gevaerd is Brazil's leading UFOlogist, editor of the country's only UFO publication, *UFO*, and the director of the Brazilian Centre for Flying Saucer Research, the largest organisation of its kind in the country. He came to international attention in 1996, through his investigation of the famous Varginha case, where two extraterrestrials were captured after their spacecraft crashed in southern Brazil.

According to Gevaerd, there were numerous UFO sightings in the first few weeks of 1996. On the night of 19 January, two people reported seeing a spacecraft which had difficulty flying. At around 7:30 a.m. on the morning of 20 January, a number of people in the town of Varginha reported spotting a humanoid creature around. It had red eyes, a reddish-brown coloured skin and three small bumps on its head. Frightened residents called the Fire Department. They located the creature in an area called Jardim Andere and called the Brazilian army. By 10:30 a.m., army personnel and firemen had managed to net the creature and placed it in a crate. They then took it to the School of the Sergeant of Arms in the nearby town of Tres Coracoes.

Gevaerd discovered that a second extraterrestrial was found later that day. Three girls saw another creature cowering by a wall not far from where the first one had been captured. They told Gevaerd that it had a large head, brown skin, thick veins on its upper body and three protuberances on its head that looked like horns. At 8:30 p.m., a military vehicle with two policemen in it almost drove over a creature Gevaerd believes was the same as the one seen by the girls. One of the officers jumped out of the truck and grabbed it with his bare hands. He held it in his lap until they reached a nearby medical facility. Gevaerd discover that the creature was later transferred to the Humanitas Hospital in Varginha. The capture of the second creature occurred on a Saturday night when everyone was out on the streets. Many people saw the commotion and military trucks pulling up. In all, Gevaerd and his fellow researchers have interviewed over forty witnesses who saw the authorities capture the two creatures.

The aliens' UFO was first detected by an American satellite and the US informed the Brazilian military as part of an agreement between the two nations. So Brazilian radar was on full alert when the craft entered Brazilian airspace and it tracked the craft until it crashed into the state of Minas Gerais. Gevaerd has proof that both the US and the Brazilian government knew immediately that a UFO had crashed and knew roughly its location. Gevaerd tried to get details but there was a complete clamp down in the military. He believes that both extraterrestrials survived the crash, but died within a few hours of capture. The crash seems to have left them badly injured. The crash had occurred at around 3 a.m. When people saw them a few hours later, they were on their last legs.

'It could have been due to the crash,' says Gevaerd. 'Or perhaps the environment was not suitable.'

Gevaerd believes the US was involved from the start. He knows the creatures were later moved to the Hospital of Clinics at the University of Campinas. They were examined by a team of doctors, headed by Brazil's leading forensic scientist, Dr Furtunato Badan Palhares. In all, fifteen masked doctors examined the creatures' bodies, and seven of the team were non-Brazilians – probably US scientists. Gevaerd also thinks that the bodies were shipped to the US. A special US transport plane arrived on 26 January at Campinas, and he thinks that the bodies were taken to an Air Force base in North America.

'Everything indicates US involvement,' says Gevaerd. 'Our government does what it's told to do by the US. They co-operate with the US in return for favours.'

Since the Varginha incident, Gevaerd has consolidated his reputation by his investigation of 'Operation Saucer'. This began in 1977 when hundreds of UFO sightings came from an area along the Amazon river. Many people said they had been attacked by beams of light. Later many of them suffered symptoms of anaemia, although it is not clear whether this was due to loss of blood or to receiving a discharge from a UFO. The state authorities sent in teams of doctors, but they were attacked too. Eventually, the central government took the problem seriously, and, in September 1977, a team of twelve men from the Brazilian Air Force were sent to the area to investigate. They collected reports from over three thousand people who had seen UFOs and had been attacked by balls of light. This inquiry was called 'Operation Saucer' and was headed by Colonel Uyrange Hollanda, who told his story to Gevaerd in 1987, shortly before committing suicide.

The Operation Saucer team were ordered to talk to witnesses, document the evidence and get photographs – they took five hundred photographs of the UFOs in all. Hollanda's team were also ordered to see if they could make contact with the aliens and ask them why they had come. Although he got no direct answer to this question, Hollanda believed that the aliens were here to collect genetic material. Attacks usually took place when victims were alone and isolated. They would see a ball of light moving towards them. It would give them an electric shock, which would put them to sleep for several hours. When they regained consciousness, they would find small scars on their bodies, which Hollanda believed were caused by the extraction of tissue samples. But the damage was not just physical. Many victims suffered trauma and many were terrified. One fisherman who was attacked repeatedly was so terrified that he broke a leg while fleeing, Gevaerd says, but continued running despite his injury.

Hollanda reported seeing the craft associated with the attacks. They were sleek and teardrop-shaped, with a large transparent area at the front, like a helicopter canopy, he told Gevaerd. On occasions, alien figures could be seen moving around inside. Towards the end of their investigations, short, humanoid, Grey aliens were regularly seen by the team. According to Gevaerd, the team's presence seemed to attract the interest of the extraterrestrials. Hollanda told Gevaerd that the aliens seemed to know everything the team did before they did it. For instance, if they decided to go up river, they would find the aliens waiting when they got there. Team members felt as though they were being observed. Eventually, the military team themselves fell victim to attacks. All members of the team were abducted. Hollanda himself was subjected to multiple abductions, during which he was examined both physically and psychologically by the aliens. He also told Gevaerd that he had acquired paranormal abilities as a result of his contacts.

However, these abductions caused Hollanda to lose his emotional stability. When Gevaerd interviewed him in July 1987, he broke down and wept. When he described his contact with the aliens he was obviously under great strain and was still plagued by strange phenomena years after he left the Amazon. He committed suicide two days before the first of a series of sessions of regressional hypnosis Gevaerd had arranged for him, thinking this might help.

Operation Saucer concluded that there was no doubt that the UFOs were responsible for the attacks. It also found that people were being abducted; some did not return. Gevaerd does not know why these abductions were happening, or why the aliens had such a special interest in the natives of the Amazon – although it is possible they conducted their experiments in this area because the people were isolated, living far from any protection.

Gevaerd finds the phenomenon of abduction a big puzzle. He has investigated cases where abductees have acquired paranormal abilities, including telepathic and healing powers, as a result. One case that Gevaerd investigated was that of Vera Lucia Guimaraes Borges, who was abducted in the 1960s when she was a teenager. She was living in the house of her grandmother in Valencia, near Rio de Janeiro, when she was woken one night by a noise and was lured into the kitchen. There she was confronted by a ball of light, which hovered in front of her. She promptly fainted. After this incident, Borges acquired remarkable paranormal powers, including the ability to diagnose a patient's illness by simply thinking about them. Under regressional hypnosis, she discovered that she had been abducted by two aliens – one male and one female in appearance – who had subjected her to a medical examination.

Doctors were called in by Gevaerd to test her diagnostic skills. She was 99 per cent accurate. One of the doctors was so impressed that he used her as a consultant. In one case, she told him that a young male patient had been bitten by a poisonous creature and told him which antidote to use.

'I know of many cases where abductees have acquired paranormal abilities,' says Gevaerd. 'Although abductions appear to have no obvious benefits, there are plenty of cases that illustrate we are visited by ETs who can help us do special things.'

However, Hollanda certainly did not benefit from his abduction, and other abductees gain nothing and end up traumatised. Although there are a lot of dedicated UFO researchers in Brazil, only a few are investigating abductions. As a result, Gevaerd is collaborating with the North American alien abduction experts Budd Hopkins and Dr John Mack, who he hopes will teach Brazilian investigators how to do abduction research.

'There is so much new data here that has not yet been seized upon by the media,' says Gevaerd. He believes that it could be the clue to an enigma: 'I'm convinced humanity, in a number of different forms, is spread out all over the universe. We are just a tiny fraction of what exists.'

Jaime Maussan

Latin America is one of the world centres of UFO activity and Mexican TV investigative journalist Jaime Maussan became interested when a huge wave of UFO sightings occurred in Mexico in 1991. He quickly became the country's leading UFOlogist. Since then he has gone on to investigate the semi-legendary, blood-sucking vampiric entity known as the Chupacabra, or 'goat-sucker'. These have attacked livestock throughout Mexico, leaving their carcasses drained of blood, and they are thought to be extraterrestrial in origin.

The first Chupacabra attack that Maussan investigated occurred on 17 July 1994. Official records show that, around this time, people were going out into the mountains to search for a mysterious creature that had been seen sucking the blood from cattle. At that time, the name 'Chupacabra' had not been coined. Maussan believes that this is important, because it shows that the attacks are a real phenomenon, not something created by the media. The media did not become interested until 1996.

Maussan's interest grew out of his UFO research. From the start they seemed to be related. When Chupacabra attacks started to happen, he began to look into them and soon found that they were a real phenomenon. This became his main area of research because it inspired even more fear in people than the UFOs.

His research has taken him to the places where the attacks have occurred and he has interviewed eyewitnesses. This led him to build up a network of investigators across the country and he corresponds with other researchers outside Mexico.

Chupacabras mostly attack sheep, but sometimes chickens and goats. Rarely, they attack larger animals such as donkeys or cattle. But least 80 per cent of the attacks Maussan has investigated were on sheep.

The animals concerned are domesticated and live close to humans. There have been no reports of attacks on deer or other large wild animals in Mexico, though Maussan has read a report of deer being attacked over the border in New Mexico. On that occasion, ten deer were attacked. However, even though they were wild animals, they were in a controlled situation. It seems that wild animals are somehow more protected from this kind of presence. Maybe they can escape and hide from the predator more easily.

The creatures in the first attacks were described as some sort of big cat with wings. The witnesses had all seen the creature close to, sometimes from just a few feet away. Then the press began reporting what was happening in Puerto Rico. In 1996, the name 'Chupacabras' was imported and hundreds of reports began.

The recent sightings are consistent. People report an animal about three feet tall with a face like a kangaroo or a mouse. It has a small, spiny back, wings, little hands and very thick feet. Some people have seen it flying. Footprints have been found and samples of what appears to be the creature's excrement have been taken. Maussan's problem is that these incidents take place far out in the country where there are no facilities to carry out an investigation. When he finds out about an attack, it is usually two, three or even four days after it has happened. By then it is too late. You need to be there straight away, he says.

Rural communities are terrified of the attacks. In one town, local people painted crosses on the walls of the buildings around the site of the attack, hoping that it would given them some form of protection. After an incident in the town of Sinaloa, the whole community was so frightened that people could not sleep. There were so many attacks that people became afraid for their children. They figured that if the creature could attack animals with impunity their children would be next. Animals were disappearing every night and people figured that it would soon take a child. They had to call in the army to get some protection. Interestingly, the attacks always took place at night. Maussan does not have any reports of attacks in Mexico that have happened during daylight.

Maussan has linked these attacks with UFO reports. Elements of the Chupacabra phenomenon suggest that creatures responsible for the attacks are coming from another world. Some people have suggested that they come from another dimension or reality. After having investigated this phenomenon, Maussan concludes that the creatures responsible are no known terrestrial species.

Humans have been attacked by Chupacabras both in Mexico and Puerto Rico. Maussan believes this may be related to the Mexican version of vampires. In Mexican folklore, people are turned into animals that suck blood from their victims. In one modern-day case a man managed to fight off a Chupacabra and escape. The struggle was witnessed by his wife and his brother. Their three accounts match. Apparently, the creature smelled very bad. The victim was left in a state of shock with two small, bloody holes in his arm.

To Maussan, this suggests that the same creature is responsible for old-fashion vampire tales and modern-day Chupacabra attacks.

'Perhaps these vampires were not human,' he says, 'and it is the same old creature that has been with us for a long time but we have never been able to discover exactly what it is.'

He has come across some cases where animals have survived for several hours after having been drained of blood. Maussan has found some strange substance left in the holes in the victims' carcasses which allows the blood to flow rather than coagulate normally. A proper chemical analysis of this substance might indicate what kind of creature is responsible for these attacks.

Maussan investigated the 1996 case, where there was an attack on some sheep in the small town of Puebla. A farmer, Dom Pedro, called the local vet, Soledad de la Pena. When she arrived she was amazed to see one of the sheep still alive, twelve hours after the attack, even though it had been drained of blood. Maussan thought this could be crucial.

'If we could find out what chemical was secreted to keep the animal alive after being drained of blood, it could be a very real and major breakthrough in medicine that could benefit mankind,' he says.

But Maussan has not been able to get this sort of work done in Mexico. Although some doctors and some universities have expressed an interest, none have come forward publicly.

Meanwhile, the authorities have been unable to explain these attacks, so they have chosen to ignore the whole phenomenon – another parallel with UFOs. And the church has refused to comment. Maussan is a little stumped about what to do next. When the Chupacabra attacks first started in Mexico, everyone was taken by surprise. By the time the media were interested, and Maussan had everything set up in order to investigate the attacks, the main spate was over. However, if the attacks start again, Maussan will be ready for them.

Dan Sherman

After twelve years in the US Air Force, Dan Sherman broke all his secrecy oaths and came forward to reveal his involvement in a super-secret National Security Agency training programme, aimed to teach him how to communicate with extraterrestrials. In just two years on the course, Sherman moved from basic extraterrestrial liaison to complex discussion concerning alien abductions.

Sherman's training began in 1992. He had been working in electronic intelligence analysis and was sent to NSA headquarters at Fort Meade, Maryland, for an intermediate electronic intelligence course, or so he thought. But when he arrived, he was told that he had been signed up to an extra training course in the evenings.

This course was part of a secret programme called 'Project Preserve Destiny'. Sherman was told that PPD had started in 1960. It was a 'genetic management' project and its purpose was to cultivate human offspring so that they would be able to communicate with the Grey-like extraterrestrials by a method they called 'intuitive communication or IC'. He was told that he and the other people chosen to work in the programme were the offspring of pregnant female abductees, whose foetuses were genetically modified during their abduction. As genetically-modified human, he already possessed the latent ability to communicate with aliens, but the course he was about to begin would heighten his IC abilities.

For ten weeks, every evening after his regular daytime training, Sherman was driven to an underground facility. There he was sat in front of a computer and trained as an 'intuitive communicator'. At the beginning of his training, he had to listen to a specific sound tone on headphones. Then he had to duplicate this tone by humming it mentally, while trying to affect the shape of a sine wave on the computer screen in front of him. This was made doubly difficult because there was no physical connection between him and the computer. Sherman believes that it must have been of a very advanced design that somehow picked up his brain wave. Anyway, after two days of trying he found he was able to flatten the sine wave.

After basic training, Sherman was moved 'PPD base 1', where he went to work with two other officers inside a 'communication van'. The work seemed like any normal electronic intelligence operation, but while on duty he received his first extraterrestrial communication. He had just powered up his equipment, when a message came into his mind. It said: 'Prepare for information string.'

Sherman followed the procedure he had learnt in training. Then after a few minutes, the alien communication began. It consisted of a string of numbers that meant nothing to him. But he typed them into his computer and sent them to the NSA for analysis. He was sure that the message came from an extraterrestrial intelligence, rather than some human psychic, because the means of communication was totally different from anything human. Psychic communication is often abstract and vague. This was clear and precise. Humans communicate in a linear mode, with a beginning and one thing coming after another until you reach the end. The alien data was non-linear. All the information was there in his head instantaneously. It was his job to interpret it and make it into a linear sequence, type it out and pass it on.

The communications would always be initiated by his alien contact, and would invariably be an array of digits. Occasionally, he would have to get the alien entity to repeat something, but essentially the communication was one-way. However, after three months, their mental communication began to broaden out. He was able to ask his contact a few questions. As he felt intuitively that the alien lacked emotion, he asked it whether it had feelings like we do. It replied that, although it had a similar emotional make-up, it was far less affected by its surroundings than we are. Beyond that, when he tried to pose more direct questions, the alien broke off communication.

Sherman was then transferred to 'PPD Base 2'. He continued to receive strings of numbers from an alien source, but he sensed his contact was a different alien being from the one he had been in contact with before. Gradually, the nature of the communication began to change. The strings of meaningless numbers became map references and they were accompanied by mental pictures. Some of the communication was launch data from unsuccessful US Shuttle and rocket launches and he could see mental pictures of where the technology had malfunctioned.

After about nine months at PPD Base 2, Sherman began to receive information that he thought related to human abductions. Terms like 'residual pain level', 'body normalisation', and 'potentiality for recall' came up. His first abduction communication also carried a map reference, which specified a location in Florida.

Sherman discovered that this contact was a Grey. It told him that Greys had been visiting Earth for a very long time. They have communicated with various civilisations throughout human history, but this has been fraught with difficulties – hence the more diffident approach they are taking today. They had also visited a large number of extraterrestrial intelligences across the universe. Although their lifespan was similar to that of humans, they were not bound by space and time as we were. That meant they could travel huge distances across the universe by manipulating time.

As enlightening as this was, Sherman had begun to feel uncomfortable with his covert work. He grew tired of being told how important he was because of his IC abilities, while being treated like an underling with no 'need to know' what the communication he was handling was all about. He left PPD in December 1994, and quit the military altogether in April 1995.

After taking extensive legal advice, Sherman sat down with Area 51 researcher Glenn Campbell and wrote the book *Above*

Black, about his experiences in the NSA's PPD programme. It was published in 1997. Since then Sherman has lectured at UFO conventions all over America and his story has been widely reported.

However, PPD is so far beyond top-secret – so far 'above black' – that it is almost impossible to verify its existence. Sherman compares security at this level to the layers of an onion. The outer skin is 'unclassified' – the activities the military get up to that the public see. Below that there is 'level five,' which he describes as 'for official use only'. This prevents ordinarily confidential information being disseminated widely. Next comes 'level four'. This is secret information which, if leaked, would threaten national security. 'Level three' is top secret where information is compartmentalised and only accessible if the right codes are used. 'Level two' is a layer of black operations that only the US President and a handful of trusted Congressmen know about. Beyond that is 'level one' where 'grey matter' and 'slanted missions' such as PPD exist and where even base commanders may not know what is going on.

To back his story sherman has produced certificates proving he was trained by the NSA in electronic intelligence. Other UFO researchers have checked out much of Sherman's story. But one – Bob Huff – has provided a whole raft of corroborating evidence.

A West Point graduate, Bob Huff retired from the US military to work as an expert in information technology in companies that were contracted to work for the Federal government and the intelligence community. He has also been investigating the military involvement in the UFO phenomenon for decades. Huff was able to verify that PPD Base 1 was the US Air Force Base in San Vito, Italy, and PPD Base 2 was Buckley AFB in Colorado. He has also been able to provide independent confirmation for the existence of PPD. One of his sources was a woman whose father was a senior marketing executive at the communications giant AT&T. He had worked on classified programmes for the intelligence community while at that company and was able to confirm the existence of PPD during a classified briefing.

Several of Huff's sources have confirmed that PPD was set up by Majestic-12, the presidential commission set up after the

Roswell incident to keep the wraps on the subject of UFOs. He has confirmed that MJ-12 is in contact with at least one species of alien, either through live contact or remote communication. From what he has been told, you cannot apply to join a group like MJ-12. They never recruit. They operate by monitoring a potential candidate's career and if he fits their criteria they bring him into the programme. Huff believes this is what happened to Sherman.

'I think there has been an invisible hand guiding his career throughout his life,' says Huff.

Huff thinks that Sherman's strange method of communication is related to remote viewing – another project the military and intelligence establishments are pursuing. Both are paranormal channels and both operate on a non-local level beyond the normal constraints of space and time. According to Huff, Sherman is able to moderate some sort of 'paranormal continuum', so his modulations, in whatever dimension the aliens operate, are detected by their technology.

Huff has checked out Sherman's story exhaustively. Although he admits that, on face value, it sounds 'pretty far out', he has accumulated enough evidence to satisfy himself that Sherman is telling the truth. If so, this confirms what many researchers have long suspected: the military really is involved in alien abductions.

Patrick Harpur

Novelist and philosopher Patrick Harpur believes that UFOs are akin to fairies, the Loch Ness monster, Yetis, Bigfoot and many other inexplicable anomalies. They are the products of what he calls 'daimonic reality' – named for the Greek daimons, otherworldly entities who mediated between mankind and the gods. They inhabit a realm that co-exists with our everyday reality, as he explains in his book, *Daimonic Reality: Understanding Otherworld Encounters*.

Daimonic reality is an intermediate world between the material and spiritual worlds. The modern psychological concept of the unconscious is a recent model of daimonic reality. This places the nether world firmly inside us. But Harpur believes that daimonic reality is not really inside us, any more than it is outside us. In fact, it is impossible to locate with any precision. It is elusive, shape-changing and incomprehensible.

Nineteenth-century Romantics called it the 'imagination'. They experienced it as a dynamic realm separate from everyday reality, which was inhabited by archetypal images and myths. The Romantic imagination derives directly from the Neoplatonists' idea of 'Soul of the World'. This lay between the world we perceive with our senses and the ideal world of forms or archetypes.

The Swiss psychologist Carl Jung rediscovered this world and called it the 'collective unconscious'. At first, under the influence of Freudian psychoanalysis, he located it inside us. But later, when he studied religions and folklore from around the world, he was forced to recognise that it lay outside us as well.

'Reality,' says Harpur, 'is always psychic, lying between us and the world, partly inside, partly outside; partly personal, partly impersonal; partly material, partly immaterial, and so on – a reality that's as ambiguous as the daimons who personify it.'

Although UFOs are the most common modern manifestation of daimonic reality, Harpur says that people still encounter fairies. Although they are slightly old-fashioned, fairies are still around. They are not reported because nobody is looking for them and people who do see them are too embarrassed to say so. Harpur wrote an article for *Country Living* magazine and invited people to write in if they had seen fairies. He received a sackful of letters. The creatures people had seen tended to be the little cherub-like entities of Victorian fairytales. No one reported seeing the classic fairies of central Europe, elves, or the *Sidhe* of Irish folklore. These were human-size and fierce, not little things with wings that sit around on flower petals.

Harpur points out that there are clear parallels between fairies and 'aliens'. It used to be fairies that abducted humans. They would steal young men to intermarry to improve their race and steal young mothers for their milk. This would now be interpreted as the alien agenda to produce human–alien hybrids. While fairies would pay us back by helping ensure the fertility of our crops and bringing us good luck in other ways, aliens provided us with a fertile crop of new technology.

Harpur believes that fairy wisdom has been 'literalised' into the aliens' advanced technology and finds the idea of delightful rural meetings with fairies more interesting than the grim exchanges that take place with the Grey aliens who bring humankind fear and pain. Harpur believes that the very sterility of the Greys reflects our own sterile view of the otherworld.

Harpur thinks that humankind needs its daimons, even today, when science tries to explain everything. This is because there has always been some form of daimon. Human beings seem to need some form of other-worldly beings to interact with. That is why, in an age when reason is supposed to prevail, half the world believes in flying saucers and aliens. You can't dispense with daimons. Because they are shapeshifters, if you try and get rid of them, they simply take another form. He thinks that it is crucial that we acknowledge daimonic reality. If we don't, the results are the same as if we seek to deny the urges of the subconscious. Freud formulated an inescapable psychological law – whatever is repressed simply reappears in another guise.

'This is as true of the daimons in the Neoplatonic Soul of the World as it is of today's unconscious complexes,' says Harpur.

The daimons always return. If you do not allow them in the outside world, they appear within as alien voices that cry out from the psychoanalyst's couch. And if you ban them from the world of nature, they come back from outer space.